Androula's Kitchen

Cyprus on a plate

To Mum & Dad

Editor: Sandy Draper
Designer: Andrew Milne

Published by Sonia Demetriou

ISBN 978-0-9574002-0-7

For more information

Email
sonia.demetriou@googlemail.com

Website
http://androulaskitchen.wordpress.com/

Facebook
https://www.facebook.com/cyprusonaplate

Androula's Kitchen

Cyprus on a plate

A meze of Cypriot culture. Crafts to Arts to Food. A feast for the eyes as well as the stomach.

SONIA DEMETRIOU

CONTENTS

INTRODUCTION

My first trip to Cyprus was in 1965 with my father when he returned to visit his homeland after a gap of more than 20 years. My impressions that first time have stayed with me, it felt very exotic to me aged 17; Cyprus had a truly Middle Eastern flavour then whereas today it has a more European feel. The journey, taking three to four days, gave me the feeling of having travelled some distance to a far-off land. We flew from London to Brindisi in Italy, where we arrived at the port in the evening to board an old rusting ferry called *The Venus*. She was notorious among frequent travellers of this route and it was to the relief of everyone when, a few years later, she gave up the fight and quietly sank.

As we embarked this worn-out old lady, we were jostled and worried noisily up the gangplank by a large group of Cypriot grannies dressed in black with scarves tied around their heads, and carrying all manner of bundled-up belongings. It seemed chaotic, no orderly queues here. The boat was very crowded not least because among the passengers and swelling the throng was a large group of good-natured Israeli scouts heading for Haifa, the ferry's final destination. They slept on the upper decks and whiled away the evenings by singing, which usually including a spirited rendition of *Hava Nagila*. My mother and I shared a four-berth cabin below deck with two of those black-clad old ladies, while my father shared a cabin with three other

men in the men's quarters. This was our home for three days, as we journeyed to LEMESOS (Limassol). Sat on a deckchair looking out to sea, you might as well have been on a five-star liner – the sun and refreshing breeze was the same and the view of the sea and sky just as endless.

Even though our sleeping quarters were fairly basic the dining room was light and airy, the food very tasty and plentiful, and the crew really friendly. After our boat had squeezed its way through the narrow passage of the impressive Isthmus of Corinth Canal –the rocky, rough-hewn sides towering above us, we stopped at Piraeus in Athens. Disembarking onto *terra firma* once more, we threaded our way through the hustle and bustle, and made full use of our brief stop to visit the ancient Parthenon.

The passage around the Isthmus can often be choppy and the boat tossed and heaved quite a bit making a considerable number of the passengers seasick. The rumour spread that sucking lemons alleviated the nausea and sour expressions became a common sight. Luckily I found the turbulence exhilarating when standing on the upper decks, although it was not so much fun below decks. On a subsequent voyage, aboard *The Venus'* successor *The Apollonia,* the air-conditioning in the dining room below deck, chose this particular point in the journey to breakdown. The combination of the heat, the rolling motion and the smell of food on that occasion proved too much for me.

FIRST IMPRESSIONS

We arrived at LEMESOS (Limassol) port late in the evening and I remember the warmth rising up from the ground to enfold us, as we disembarked, and the fragrant smell of the air. I have noticed wherever you go in Cyprus there is a sweet smell in the air, due to the many herbs and flowers growing wild everywhere and never far away is the mouthwatering smell of SOUVLAKIA floating on the breeze.

The taxi ride to my father's village just outside LEFKOSIA (Nicosia) took a while. I have a vivid memory of the headlights lighting up the silvery bark and leaves of the Eucalyptus trees, giving them a ghostly appearance in the dark, the almost deafening sound of crickets, the dusty roads, the music coming from radios, as we passed KAFENEIA, with wailing BAZOUKIES and voices full of longing and melancholy, which tugged at my heart – their message clear even though the words were incomprehensible; very different to the sixties pop I was used to hearing. It was August, the heat was fierce, intensifying the scents and smells of the earth, as well as the wonderful aromas of jasmine, gardenia and … goats.

The way of life in the village, YEROLAKKOS, was very different to the life we had left behind in London, and fundamentally it had been the same way for centuries. Most of my relatives kept chickens for eggs

and meat, and used clay ovens outside. Traditional dishes such as KLEFTIKO and TAVA were cooked in a small oven and a large one was used for breads. My aunt Maritsa and her husband George kept a herd of goats and made HALLOUMI and ANARI, the Cypriot cheeses, from the milk. Another aunt, Eugenia had a loom on which she wove cloth for sheets, napkins, and so on. My female cousins spent their spare time sitting in the yard working on either embroidery or crocheting with a very fine hook that made your eyes water with the effort of trying to see the stitch. Uncle Andrew, as well as being the barber, also kept one of the coffee shops with a television, there were very few in the village then. This was the domain of the men, where they would drink coffee or brandy, talk, argue and play TAVLI (backgammon). Uncle Nicholas was the shoemaker and Uncle Christopher was the shopkeeper of one of the three PANTOPOLEIA (grocers' shops), which sold every conceivable item a householder would need, with sacks of dried and fresh goods ranged outside and inside around the shop and the shelves stacked high with goods. Uncle Christopher lived with his family in part of the original family house. Built in the traditional style, the main dwelling was in the middle with buildings ranged either side of a courtyard. The main building had a wide covered terrace in front with stone arches. When my father returned to the family home that first time it was as if the 'Prodigal Son' had returned and although I don't remember the killing of a fatted calf exactly, we certainly had, what looked to me, like a banquet laid out on a long table in this courtyard surrounded by all the family and more on the periphery. The Cypriots are in their element when providing food for guests and my Aunt Maria was a fabulous cook. It seemed to me that everybody there was related to us by some connection, however far removed. Cyprus is an island that works more like a village and, wherever you go in the world, when you meet a fellow Cypriot they ask where your family comes from and more often than not, they will know someone – a relative or friend – that lives in your village or comes from there.

The things I really missed during my stay were a bathroom and a comfy chair to flop in. Most homes only had the one kind of seating, the KAREKLA (chair), which is upright and hard. The artistry of sitting comfortably on one of these is to have three: one to sit on, one at your side on which to rest your arm, the third in front of you serving a dual purpose – the seat is used to rest your coffee tray and the rails to rest your feet.

In 1993, a few years before my father died, he returned to live in Cyprus, as many Cypriots that live abroad wish to do. He chose a beautiful spot near the sea and he used this time of reflection to write down the events of his life as he remembered them, and given me an insight into how he lived his early life in this village for which I will always be grateful.

DAD'S EARLY YEARS

His parents were farmers in an agricultural community and were comfortably placed by local standards, owning 400 acres of arable land, 200 goats and sheep, and four oxen. He was the eldest child of 12 children of whom only eight survived. It is clear that he dearly loved his mother who obviously had a hard life with so many children to care for, as well as all the duties of a farmer's wife. At harvest-time there could be up to a dozen extra workers on the farm that all needed feeding and my grandmother would single-handedly cook and bake for them.

His father was stern with the family, although they rarely saw him as he worked in the fields all day and spent his evenings in the coffeehouse. Although my father was an enthusiastic and able scholar further education would have incurred expense and my grandfather thought he would be of more use on the farm, and so at 12 he left school. He started by learning to plough: pulled by two oxen it was a tough thing to master when he could barely see above the handles. But his perseverance paid off and gradually he was given more and more responsibilities and by 17 he was running the farm and my grandfather was able to spend his days, as well as his evenings, leisurely in the coffeehouse. The younger siblings had their parts to play as they grew but dad, being the eldest, was expected to support the family. When there was no farming to be done he earned money doing odd jobs.

My Dad aged 21

My Granny & Grandad and some of the family

Every two or three years there was a drought and the crops barely yielded enough seed corn for the following year let alone for food, so aged 19 he decided to increase his earnings. He collected all his savings and bought himself a mule and cart and put himself out for hire to transport goods. He, along with some friends, secured a contract to transport stone from a nearby quarry to the builders in LEFKOSIA (Nicosia) 6.4km away. Later, he won a contract to ferry hard core for a new road being built from LEFKOSIA to MORFOU. The work was hard but he found it pleasant and it paid quite well.

As the mule pulled the cart along on his journeys homeward after a hard day's work, he would sit and daydream. His ambition was to travel although he only spoke colloquial Greek and hadn't even travelled as far as the sea on his own island! My grandmother however, had two brothers living abroad, one in England where he planned to go first as a stepping-stone to visit the other in the USA where he wanted to settle eventually. He planned to travel with a friend and after lengthy discussions they formed a plan. He sold the mule and cart and all his other possessions to pay for his passage on an old steamer, a suit (his first ever matching jacket and trousers) and to obtain a passport and documents. Naturally the family was distraught when they learned of his imminent departure, but he was determined to leave Cyprus. It was 1934 when my father left Cyprus and he never made it to America as events overtook him – he met my mother in London.

Left My cousins at their needlework

Right The view across TREIS ELIES from Androula's balcony

THE LOSS OF A TRADITIONAL WAY OF LIFE

The Turkish invasion in 1974 shattered the peaceful way of life for ΥΕΡΟΛΑΚΚΟΣ and many other villages. Today most of my relatives are now living an urban city life in ΛΕΦΚΟΣΙΑ, which is very different to the village lives of their past. Progress marched briskly into the lives of Cypriots particularly after Cyprus joined the European Union in 2004.

This was made apparent to me during a visit to my cousin in the mountain village of Treis Elies in 2009, and I realised how fast the traditions of Cyprus were disappearing; the old ways of doing things getting lost in the wake of modern technology and a contemporary way of living. My cousin Androula established ΤΟ ΣΠΙΤΙΚΟ ΤΟΥ ΑΡΧΟΝΤΑ in 2005 with the aim of offering eclectic tourism that protects both the natural and social environment. She promotes the traditional foods and products made by the villagers from produce cultivated and grown in the area. By encouraging visitors to use and partake of the local facilities and products it allows the village to continue to grow and thrive. Mountain villages like ΤΡΕΙΣ ΕΛΙΕΣ are gradually losing their younger generations to the cities where more opportunities and a faster pace of living await, so many of their traditions are being lost. At the time of writing the population of ΤΡΕΙΣ ΕΛΙΕΣ is 57, its highest recorded population was more than 400 in 1946.

It was witnessing the loss of this traditional way of life that gave me the idea of recording some of the traditional foods and culinary techniques, which have been handed down through the generations. Although I have no doubt that of all the things that may disappear, traditional food is not one of them – Cypriots love their food. Some of the foodstuffs that were once commonly made at home, however, are now more commonly bought ready made from the supermarket.

Androula's kitchen is filled with the everyday objects and furniture, which, for centuries, were found in every villager's home. I love old things; anything that shows it has been used and lovingly handled over the years, and particularly everyday handcrafted objects. As I gazed around the room I wondered whether the myriad of traditional skills were still alive and well in Cyprus and how are they evolving, or are many of them getting tossed aside in the rush to join the rest of world in the bright, shiny 21st century?

These thoughts inspired me to set off and discover the answers and this book is a record of my journey in search of some of the island's local traditions and crafts, which have been integral to the Cypriot way of life for centuries. It is a tale of the people I met, the food we made and enjoyed in Androula's kitchen, and some of the Cypriots' best-loved recipes, which I collected along the way. The ancient history of Cyprus is well documented; I wanted to find out about the mundane life of yesterday and its place in modern Cyprus.

Androula's Kitchen

Androula's kitchen is found in a traditional mountain house, TO SPITIKO TOU ARCHONTA in the village of *Treis Elies* in the Troodos Mountains. The original part of the house was built more than 100 years ago and consists of one large room, which was used for living, and two adjacent rooms for storage and stables, now converted into a bedroom and bathroom. Stepping into the room with its flagstone floor, plastered walls, wooden beamed ceiling and deep recessed windows you have the feeling of being in authentic Cyprus. The open fireplace cuts across one corner and the mantle shelf is lined with an eclectic mixture of traditional and contemporary pots and jars, which have been collected over the years.

Left *Androula's tavas pot made by a local potter*

Gazing around the room the same is true of the furniture, there are the ubiquitous Cypriot KAREKLES with their rush seats; these ones are beautiful antiques with a more delicate design than their chunky machined modern counterpart, the backs and legs having a slightly irregular round shape, hand carved from walnut. Next to them sits a very comfortable rocking chair, the seat and back woven in sea-grass, made locally by a friend and chairmaker in the next village. A traditional cupboard, the top half of which has shelves with a glass door, houses precious old cups and glasses displayed on a white embroidered cloth. On the opposite side of the room, a large cupboard, crowned with a carved frieze, is used as a linen-press. This piece came with the house and was made, as part of the bride's dowry, for the newly married couple that moved into the house when it was first built. The original owners of the house, as many villagers of their day, would have had very little in the way of furniture, just the basics. Apart from the table, chairs and cupboards there would have been a SENDUKI (dowry chest) containing the new bride's linen and clothes, painstakingly made over many years in anticipation of the most important day of her life, her wedding and carried to her new home on the wedding day. The contents and appearance of these varied according to the prosperity of the family. The most humble would have been made from the stalks of the wild fennel plant, ANATHRIKA, which are as thick as your forearm but hollow, strapped together with the tendrils of the terebinth tree. Brides

from wealthy families would have had an elaborately carved ΣΕΝΔUΚΙΛ made from cypress wood; the carvings contained religious symbols and sometimes carved by ecclesiastical carvers called ΤΛΛΙΛΔΟΡΟΙ. There was, of course, also a bed usually made from iron with brass finials, beautifully dressed with linen or cotton and sometimes with silk hangings and a canopy, woven and embroidered by the bride.

Lining the walls near the stove in Androula's kitchen are baskets of various shapes and sizes housing sugar, flour, rice, beans and vegetables. A board about 2m long with even hollows along its length that was traditionally used for baking bread called a ΡΙΝΛΚΟΤΙ now accommodates a selection of nuts, oranges and lemons in its hollows. This lies

next to a ΤΣΕΣΤΟΣ, a flat broad round basket, used for drying freshly picked herbs. Lining the shelf above the stove are jars filled with all manner of dried herbs collected from Androula's garden and the surrounding countryside: rosehips jostling with mint, oregano and thyme in easy reach for brewing a custom-made cup of tea depending on the need of the hour. Traditionally here, as in many remote and rural areas without the proximity of professional medical advice, herbs were used frequently as remedies. The beneficial properties of many of the herbs are known universally: chamomile or rosemary for relief of tension, mint as a digestive aid, sage and lavender with wide-ranging anti-fungal and antiseptic properties. Cypriot herbs have a very high concentration of volatile oil often up to 33 per cent

due to the lack of water in their environment. Even today there are many grannies around the island that know just the herbal remedy for everyday ailments.

The large terrace outside has breathtaking views of surrounding Troodos (mountains) heavily wooded with pine and cedar. Traditionally this space is where all the work was done, but it now contains a long table and chairs, with large and small clay pots filled with geraniums lining the walls. Sitting in the corner there is a huge clay pot, looking very much like the ones in the Ali Baba story, big enough to hide a boy; this is a PITHARI, one of many that came with the house, and were originally used to store wine. Along one side of the terrace are further rooms that were added as the family grew and even later another storey was added, providing a spacious living area together with two large bedrooms and a bathroom. The upper floor is reached from the terrace by an outside staircase taking you up to a wooden balcony looking out over the village rooftops.

There are gardens on the outskirts of the village, which are terraced up the hillside, where a wide and plentiful array of fruits is grown. Apples, plums, cherries, walnuts, pears, vines, pomegranate, strawberries, olives, almonds and so the list goes on. Cyprus is blessed with fertile soil and a warm climate, and almost anything grows here. Many herbs grow wild in the hedgerows and villagers still forage for them, as well as wild greens when they are in in season, to cook and eat.

Right View from Androula's terrace

Androula has one of these gardens and the bank is so steep you have to use a ladder from the path in order to reach it. When she first moved to TREIS ELIES her parents visited and took her along the hedgerows showing her and naming the different wild greens that she could pick to eat. The path here, located at the north end of the village near the road to KAMINARIA, is the beginning of a nature trail that takes you along the side of the river known as The Dragon, a tributary of the DIARIZOS and over the TREIS ELIES Venetian Bridge. There are several of these bridges still surviving locally, which were built by the Venetians to enable pack animals, mainly camels, to cross the river with their loads of copper from the mines in Troodos to PAFOS (Paphos). The variety and beauty of nature here is a wonder to behold, with the river rushing over the rocks below, the birds singing in the trees above and all around rustling, dappled, dense and multi-layers of green.

Roses grow in abundance here and Androula has many in her gardens, which she picks daily when in flower. Not because they look and smell beautiful, which they do of course, but to pluck the petals which are then left to dry. To destroy something so lovely in its prime and leave the petals scattered to shrivel and dry seems like senseless vandalism but this means they can be preserved and put to good use as a refreshing tea or sprinkled in the bath where they give off a relaxing, sensuous scent. The damask rose has a deep pink colour and a luxuriously rich, warm

Left The Dragon tributary of The Diarizos river

scent and the smell wafts towards you as you walk into her house. Roses are thought to be the first flower ever cultivated by man and have been held in high regard since ancient times by many cultures. One of the many myths surrounding the bloom is that the tears of Aphrodite, mingled with the blood of her lover Adonis after he was wounded, creating the red rose and forever to be known as a symbol of love. Roses have antibiotic qualities and can be used as a sedative, as well as to combat constipation or provide an excellent skin cleanser. Rose water is often used in cookery in Cyprus and many village women would distill their own rosewater from the damask rose petals, as well as using them to make a preserve, which served a dual purpose: a delicious sweet to eat as well as a remedy for seeing-off any pesky intestinal worms.

Nearby AGROS is well known for its roses and has a small factory, which makes many products from their harvest, not just rosewater but attar of roses, which is the essential oil used in making perfume.

Below Kelefos Bridge

LIVESTOCK

Every village family in the past would have kept chickens, pigeons, rabbits, a goat or two for milk, a pig to be fattened for its meat and, of course, a beautiful long-eared Cypriot donkey, of which like many others I am very fond. A donkey trudging up the hills laden with either his owner or the produce garnered from the fields used to be a common sight but now the donkey has been largely replaced by another kind of horsepower found under the bonnet of a truck. The donkeys in Cyprus are usually large and handsome and are not an indigenous breed. Known as the 'Mercedes of donkeys', they are similar to the donkeys found in France and Spain, and there is a theory that this donkey was brought over with the Crusaders. Until recently donkeys were very important to villagers. Before the roads were massively improved to accommodate the ever-increasing number of tourists that boosted the economy, donkeys were often the only form of transport available to carry tools and produce along the rough mountain tracks and roads to the uncompromising fields and vineyards. Uncomplaining and cheap to feed they laboured unceasingly, ploughing fields, working the olive press, pumping water from the well, when it would be blindfolded to encourage it to walk in unending circles.

The donkey population has declined as the family truck has increased in popularity, but at their height there were approximately 50,000 on the island. Today the number is probably less than 2,000, although the donkey is still indispensable for reaching the vineyards situated on steep mountainsides. In the north along the KARPASIA peninsula donkeys now run wild and are protected by the Turkish Cypriot authorities. In 1974 their owners fleeing the Turkish invasion abandoned them and have thrived and multiplied in their newfound freedom. In the south many donkeys were led to pasture when there was no longer a use for them. A donkey sanctuary in Vouni was set up in 1994 by an English couple when they were asked to look after a donkey belonging to an old couple that could no longer take care of him. Gradually the numbers of donkeys they were asked to re-home increased and the Friends of the Cyprus Donkey was set up. The founders of the sanctuary have now retired and The Donkey Sanctuary (Cyprus) continue the work they started, giving shelter to two donkeys a week on average; they now care for about 120 donkeys.

To see a donkey on a mountain track is, for me, part of the very fabric of the island, it seems in tune with nature and the landscape. In these days of awareness about carbon footprints, the donkey's footprint is surely preferable to the petrol-guzzling 4x4 trucks that zoom along the roads?

In the northwest of Cyprus lies the last bastion of untouched wild nature that is the AKAMAS

Right *Warning! If you stay
In TREIS ELIES never ask for
a remedy for drunkenness,
although it sobers you up
miraculously quickly, it
involves drinking tea made
from dried donkey excrement!
It is a special remedy of the
village apparently.*

peninsula, but it is constantly under threat from people who want to exploit this very fact. Safari trips regularly cross this rocky terrain using Land Rovers, which may offer the passengers the thrill of excitement but at what cost to the immediate environment and its inhabitants? What better way to see the wonderful flora and fauna of this area of outstanding natural beauty, than from astride the gently moving back of a donkey? Travelling this way it is possible to connect with the landscape in a far more immediate way, and with time to notice the butterflies and birds, and smell the wonderful aromatic air. None of these things can be enjoyed from inside a noisy, dusty vehicle.

I came across a couple of tour companies that have had the same idea and, by developing a

new purpose for the local donkeys, they also give visitors a unique experience. One excursion, which particularly caught my eye, was from a donkey farm in KALOKEDARA to visit the remote monastery of PANAYIA TOU SINDHI, and it struck me that this is the perfect way of viewing this beautifully restored building.

Toward the end of my visit in 2009 I came across a sign for this monastery and, having previously read about it, decided spontaneously, to follow the signpost. Since Cyprus has joined the E.U all the roads have been greatly improved and this makes driving very much easier than it used to be but also takes away the slight sense of adventure when faced with a rough track to navigate. The road I followed to take me to PANAYIA TOU SINDHI very soon turned into just such a track. It snaked and turned down the hillside, getting dustier and rougher by the minute and it seemed to go on forever. Tantalizingly I caught

glimpses of the monastery down in the valley and then around the next bend it would disappear only to reappear around the next. The landscape was very open, only the deep golden stubble of the harvested wheat lay ahead and there were no trees breaking the horizon. Eventually I came to the bottom of the valley and the road suddenly stopped as it reached the narrow riverbed, which of course was bone dry. Here the ground dipped and a few large flat stones had been laid over a culvert to allow vehicles to cross and then the track became a stony path covered in wild scrub. Here I paused as I was driving an ordinary saloon car unsuitable for such terrain and reluctantly and very precariously, turned round and went back the way I came. The only thing to show for my efforts was a car covered in a thick film of dust inside and out. I later discovered that I could have walked there in 10 minutes from this spot. Next time I decide to visit PANAYIA TOU SINDHI I will choose the donkey.

THE PEOPLE OF TRIES ELIES

Arts & Crafts

Baskets

I've always loved baskets. They have a tactile quality together with the sweet, earthy smell of the natural material, whether made from cane, rush, twigs or palm leaves, and I find the intricate pattern created by the weaving very appealing. I am fascinated by the variety of styles, patterns and techniques used by basket makers all over the world. The materials are the same, supplied by nature and readily available, and with very little preparation these can be employed to produce a vast array of baskets of all shapes and sizes with all manner of uses. As a child I was in awe of my father when he made two shopping baskets, one from willow and another using plaited raffia. I still have them some 50 years later.

Left *Three small TALARIA baskets hanging with basket made from plaited palm leaves in Rosie's house*

I have since learned that basket making was very common all over Cyprus until very recently, nearly every man, woman and child had these skills, as baskets were an essential part of daily life. This is one of the oldest crafts alive today and the methods used have not altered over the years. Evidence of hard-reed baskets has been found at archaeological sites dating back to the Neolithic period, proving their surprising durability. I am impressed by the ingenuity of ancient man to invent a method whereby a stalk or twig could be turned into a useful container. Baskets, as well as being practical, are enormously aesthetically pleasing and to my delight I found that there were many different techniques and materials used in Cyprus.

DIFFERENT TYPES OF BASKETS WERE MADE FOR PARTICULAR PURPOSES:

FARTI – used for carrying light produce.

ZEMBILIA – made from soft plaited materials for olive crops. Also used as a seed basket with a long strap attached to enable the farmer to sling it over his shoulder and scatter seeds easily in the fields.

SIRIZES – double baskets from cane were slung over a donkeys back and used for transporting salt from the lakes.

KOFINI – hard cane baskets used for collecting and transporting grapes.

KOROKLIOS – small baskets with lids used by the workers in the fields to transport their lunch of cheese and olives.

TAPATZIA – mostly made from string and raffia and hung from the kitchen ceiling to store bread.

KOUKORKES – tall cylindrical hard cane baskets with a small opening at the top used for carrying chickens and other birds to market or local fairs.

TALARIA – still used today for pressing the soft cheese ANARI.

TSESTOS – made from straw and raffia into a flat broad basket and used for drying foods and grains in the sun among many other uses.

The materials used in basket making are reed cane and rushes such as the spiny rush (Juncus Acutus), plume grass or pampas grass (Erianthus), the Scirpus family of rushes: bullrush and club grass, as well as date palm leaves.

The most accessible and easiest material is reed cane, because it is very flexible when wetted. The familiar hard baskets with coloured sections, seen around the island, are made with this method. The

Top small TSESTOI
Middle SIRIZES
Bottom KOURKORKES with KOFINI
Far Right small KOURKORKES

Left Walking sticks & baskets made with twigs and cane by Elpiniki's husband

colours were originally achieved by using natural dyes but chemical colour dyes are used today. The plentiful supplies of canes means that it is also used in the ceilings of traditional houses where it is split and woven and lines the ceiling in between the beams. Villages that are known for basket making are TROULLI, LIVATHKIA, AKROTIRI, LIOPETRI and PARALIMNI.

The rushes for making soft baskets are mainly found in TROULLI, LIVATHKIA and AKROTIRI. Baskets made from plaited strips of rushes and reeds, and in some cases also from plaited leaves of date palms, were used to transport delicate crops such as olives. Baskets made of cane, reeds and twigs were used to transport heavier crops such as potatoes and still are used in some areas for collecting grapes and for straining wine.

Raffia and rope made from straw were used for making a variety of items and the techniques using these materials were developed in the KARPASIA and MESAORIA areas, spreading to the rest of the island as far as PAFOS. The PAFOS district is famous for making tsestos, circular tray-like baskets of varying sizes and with many uses, and they are decorated with brightly coloured fabrics instead of the more usual coloured straw. Traditionally they were used for drying PHIDHE, TRAHANA, and the Cypriot pasta called TRIN, and also for keeping bread and FLAOUNES. Most importantly they were used for carrying the KOULOURIA around the village, which served as an invitation to a wedding, and for carrying and displaying the bride's dowry during the wedding celebrations. These, above all other forms of basketry in Cyprus, are where the maker can express his or her creativity, the variations in colours and patterns make them not just a practical but an extremely decorative item, which can be displayed with pride on a whitewashed wall when not in use.

In some areas baskets are made using reeds together with flexible twigs from trees and bushes such as the terebinth, mulberry, olive and monk's (chaste) tree. In the villages of the LAONA district such as KRITOU TERRA, baskets were made from twigs, but sadly this method is no longer practiced as the last remaining basket maker using this technique died in 2009. However, in the village of KAMINARIA near TREIS ELIES my cousin took me to visit Elpiniki, known locally for making a traditionally smoked ham called CHOIROMERI, and she showed me some baskets her husband made using cane and twigs. He also makes some fine walking sticks out of local wood. While we were looking at his work, a very attractive stick made out of a pomegranate branch took my fancy, it had a naturally occurring pronged end, which, my brother pointed out when I gave it to him, would come in handy for trapping any snakes that he came across while walking in the countryside. Twigs and also plaited rush are used to make dressings for glass containers not only to protect the glass from damage but also the contents from the light. These containers are used for storing oil, wine and ZIVANIA, a local firewater made out of the grape skins, which are left after winemaking.

High up on the edge of the beautiful wilderness of the AKAMAS Peninsula, situated on the northwest coast in the LAONA district, is the small village of INEA. Here I went in search of a basket museum, which I first visited eight years earlier. The museum is housed in the renovated old schoolhouse in the square, opposite the church. A lovely old olive tree outside offered welcome shade while I paused to drink coffee and chat with Georgina Manolis the curator and enjoy the spectacular view of the landscape. The museum houses a small shop, which is one of the best places on the island, in my opinion, to buy a variety of baskets and other local crafted goods, including some woven and carved pieces. Among the items on sale are delightful small baskets made of soft plaited rush with lids that, in the past, were used to store olives. I use mine to store garlic. This small, interesting museum has a collection of both old and new examples of the baskets mentioned previously. Baskets, particularly TSESTOI can also be found to buy in the town of YEROSKIPOU also in the PAFOS district, which is still well known for basket making.

I wanted to see the baskets being made and thought I would soon come across someone making a basket in their front yard. How wrong I was. We visited LIOPETRI, a village near a river mouth in the

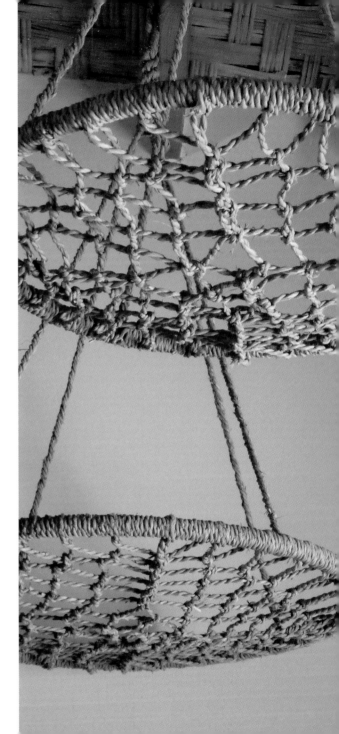

Right TAPATZIA *used for storing bread*

LARNAKA area, where I understood basket making was still a familiar sight. After some searching with my sister-in-law Angela driving us up and down the streets in search of this elusive sight, I eventually gave in and asked at the petrol station if they knew of anyone. After a telephone call to a friend, the assistant gave us directions to a lady in the village. We lost our bearings several times but were saved from endlessly going around in circles by a group of ladies, who were enjoying a pleasant afternoon chat in their yard, where we stopped to ask directions again. Our rescuer decided to accompany us by hopping in the car and directing us from the rear. This proved very useful on two counts, the second being that she saved me the trouble of explaining all over again when we finally met the elusive basket maker. It turned out that she is the now the only person in this area that still makes baskets, unluckily for me, however, she was not making any that day, as there had been a family wedding that week. Very obligingly, however, she searched around the house and showed me a selection of baskets that she had made and very lovely they were, too. As a bonus on saying goodbye, Angela and I were given some wedding biscuits to take away with us.

Sadly I didn't have time to return to LIOPETRI to see her in action but I had better luck in MESOYIE near PAFOS. Georgina gave me the name of the woman that supplies baskets to the museum shop. The only information I had was that she lived in MESOYIE

and her name was Eleni. Her house was easily recognised, however, by the long cane reeds that served as a fence. I approached the house tentatively as I didn't see any activity anywhere. As I rounded the corner of the house into the yard, I saw a man and woman sitting down having coffee. I explained in my limited Greek that I hoped to see baskets being made and they assured me after they would begin basket making again after their coffee. After inviting me to sit they asked me if I would like coffee – almost as if they had been expecting me – they pointed to a Greek coffee waiting on the tray. The coffee break over Eleni began making a basket using green cane, which had been split and soaked to make it pliable. She started by laying out several canes in a star shape on the ground, each cane intersecting the others in the centre. Then, while holding down the centre with her foot, she started to thread two other canes over and under each cane in turn around the small centre until

they were all secured and the circle complete. She continued weaving for a few more rounds until the required base width was reached. It was a laborious process and hard on the fingers. I watched until Eleni gathered up the canes to start weaving the sides and then I left her in peace. She is also the only one in her area who is now making baskets and supplies various shops as well as the museum.

During my research, I discovered a very interesting website cyprusonfilm.com where you can watch short video clips on all the Cyprus crafts, including basket making as well as traditions and history.

The Handicraft Centre In LEFKOSIA on certain days runs workshops in making TSESTOI. This centre was set up by the Republic of Cyprus' Ministry of

Left Baskets made in Liopetri

Right Eleni making her basket

Commerce and Industry in 1975 to help refugees from the north displaced by the Turkish invasion in1974. Areas that are now occupied by Turkish troops had been the home of some of the most important folk art traditions and handicrafts, weaving, pottery, lace making, etc., and consequently the exponents of these crafts were displaced to the south. LAPITHOS was the home of potters for centuries, while MESAORIA was a centre for baskets and weaving. The Handicraft Centre was a way of preserving the folk art of Cyprus and its culture, as well as giving the refugees employment by providing them with the necessary materials to produce their handicrafts and then selling the finished products to provide them with an income. The bulk of the items produced were originally embroidered and woven articles, today the Handicraft Centre houses carvers, potters, coppersmiths, silversmiths, metal workers, leatherworkers, basket weavers and garment makers. Anyone interested in learning one of these skills can take part in experimental workshops run by the centre. There is also a shop selling these crafts.

At a time when traditions and crafts were gradually disappearing, due to modernisation of the commercial and agricultural systems, the Turkish invasion caused a revival of interest in folk art traditions and handicrafts and secured a tentative future for them. Even the darkest cloud has a silver lining it seems.

Left Shadow puppet

Right The Handicraft Centre in Lefkosia

Weaving

Weaving and embroidery were part of every woman's life in the past. Even as recently as 40 years ago my Aunt was weaving her own sheets and my cousins producing intricate embroidery and crocheted lace. When village life was more confined and villagers therefore had to be more self-sufficient the material for their clothes and undergarments, as well as all household linen was made by the women of the house. They would gather the raw materials, cotton, silk and wool, which was abundant on the island, prepare and weave them. Decoration and refinement was added with embroidery and lace.

Left Weaving by Rolandos

Nearly every household owned a loom and the girls of the house, with their mother's help would start to make their trousseaus as early as 10 years of age. On the wedding day textiles produced by, and handed down through, the family, would be proudly displayed around the house. This was a time when the community's estimation of a woman was gauged by her skill at the loom. In a rural community, where income was quite often unpredictable and precarious, weaving was an important way of earning extra money.

Cotton, silk and flax were all cultivated widely, my cousin Michael can remember the whole family gathering at the cotton harvest in the fields near VEROLAKKOS. There were, of course, sheep and goats to provide the wool. My father told me he kept silk worms when he lived in the village and that he fed them on the leaves of the mulberry tree; this was a widespread occupation at that time. When I was a little girl, there was great excitement one Christmas when we were sent a parcel from Cyprus. When we opened the box it contained a large bag of shelled almonds, a jar of tiny pickled birds (a delicacy in those days but now illegal), some SOUSHOUKO, a pair of handmade shoes for my father - made by my uncle Nicholas - and a silk handkerchief woven by my aunt with an embroidered edge, which I still have. Every part of the silk cocoon was used. The cocoons were boiled to get the silk thread and then cut with small scissors to make shapes, which were used to make a kind of collage embroidery of flowers and leaf designs that were placed on a black velvet background and used to make photo frames and pictures; the worms were used by the fisherman as bait. Very fine silks, taffetas and gauzes were produced in the past and so much silk was available that it was common for sheets to be made using silk as well as clothing. Sadly silk is no longer produced on the island although there was still one 76-year-old

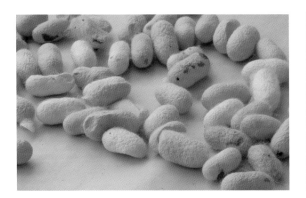

Far left silk cocoons
Left Collage made with cocoon shells

woman in LARNAKA who was still producing silk in 2006. The Cyprus Handicraft Centre were breeding a few worms when I visited, but as a curiosity rather than for producing silk. They do, however, display, some very fine examples of traditional clothing including fine shifts and blouses with detailed embroidery and beautiful skirts with bands of shimmering colour. The triangular prism structure of the fibre refracts incoming light at different angles creating its wonderful lustre and shimmering effect.

At the time of the Crusaders, Cyprus became an important centre for weaving, and produced textiles of an impressive quality and richness, which became famous throughout Europe. Large weaving workshops were established in AMMOCHOSTOS (Famagusta) and LEFKOSIA. I still have some sheets in pale yellow and white striped cotton in a seersucker weave, which I bought many years ago in LEFKOSIA but such workshops no longer exist.

Quite by chance, in the back streets of central LEFKOSIA, I came across Orphanos, a traditional costume maker. Here you can buy all the components necessary to clothe yourself from head to foot in the traditional manner. The women's traditional dress looked very comfortable, so much so that Angela and I were both tempted to buy an outfit, but resisted. It consisted of pantaloons worn under a shift with a heavier striped cotton coat, the SAYIA, worn over the top and the essential headscarf. You can even buy

the coined necklaces, pendants and earrings, which used to be part of the traditional costume. Some of the men's waistcoats were beautifully embroidered. There was a particularly dashing red jacket, which was almost completely covered with silver thread embroidery. In the villages, a man's waistcoat would usually be embroidered by his sweetheart or wife but in towns they were made by professional tailors. The men wore VRAKA, a cross between a kilt and breeches, which ended at the knee; made of coarse blue or black dimity, heavily pleated with a bustle at the back, which was tucked into the belt. The dying of the heavy woven cloth was done by the POYATZIDES (local dyers). I can remember a time when it was still a common sight in the country to see men wearing VRAKA with a pair of black knee-length leather boots and a white heavy cotton shirt under a waistcoat. In fact when I met my Grandfather on that first trip he was wearing just such attire. George Orphanos the proprietor of this emporium owned a textile factory in KERYNIA (Kyrenia) as well as a leather goods factory in STROVOLOS before the Turkish invasion. When he became displaced he decided to concentrate on his passion for making traditional outfits, which had only been a small part of his business before. He was given permission by a museum in LEFKOSIA to access and copy the original costumes in their collection. His garments are now generally bought for festivals and used by traditional dance troupes or Cypriots living abroad, sentimental for their homeland.

Weaving is another craft that has existed on the island since ancient times. Again in the LAONA district in the village of DROUSHIA, I found a museum dedicated to weaving where many lovely examples can be viewed. There were a wide variety of patterns and techniques used across the island, each area having its own speciality. One that was common was a style that used coloured wools to make a pattern in the weaving, which is widely known as FYTHKIOTIKA. It is still practiced today in the village of FYTI from where it derives its name. The patterns are mostly geometric and individual weavers would create their own designs, each with its own story. The weaving of this highly attractive fabric can be seen in action, executed by Theanou Mavrellis who, together with her husband, runs the Folk art museum at FYTI. Weaving practices have always been passed down from mother to daughter but now the traditions are in danger of being lost. In FYTI, as in so many villages, the numbers of inhabitants are dwindling and the younger generation is moving away. In 2010 three enterprising artists, Maura McKee a weaver from Northern Ireland, Sarah Dixon from London and Lauren McHugh, a weaver from Ireland, visited FYTI and met with the local weavers and, being sympathetic to their plight, decided to do something about it. Together with the people of FYTI and the LAONA Foundation, which is a non-profit private organization established to implement rural regeneration and conservation, Sara, Maura and Lauren have been developing

Left Traditional costumes at Orphanos

a strategy to help raise awareness of this once universally practiced craft. Their aim is to conserve the wealth of weaving knowledge and re-invigorate the weaving traditions of FYTI. A movement has been set in motion to initiate interest from artists, weavers, academics and universities in Cyprus and abroad, spreading the word via the Internet. One of their aims is to have weaving incorporated into a Cyprus university syllabus, encouraging artists to embrace the medium, to be innovative and progressive. Since this collaboration was started, VOUFA, a FYTI based organisation set up to promote and foster cultural and environmental activities in the village and the local area, is actively promoting weaving and the people who practice it. They offer classes and have rented a venue in the village square. They have set up a website to promote this initiative, which is updated regularly with their progress (details are listed at the back of the book).

Although much rarer than it used to be you can still find individual weavers elsewhere. There is an old woman in NEO CHORIO near POLIS in the main street, whose door is always open so that you may see her as she weaves and another woman in INEA supplies the museum shop with woven items.

Left Mrs. Mavrellis at her loom in Fyti

Top far right FYTHKIOTIKA at Fyti
Near top right & bottom Yialoussa Loom

I came across a shop in LEFKOSIA, called Yialoussa Loom in the LAIKI GEITONIA district, an area of restored traditional urban buildings, where a woman is at her loom most days weaving woollen and cotton items. The shop is stacked to the ceiling with all manner of woven and embroidered items for sale. The loom is the same one the weaver has used since she was 14 years old and which she brought with her when she was displaced from her home in the KARPASIA. There is an array of striped cotton rugs in the shop in many different colour combinations and there is something to suit every taste. This type of cotton rug is produced widely all over the island. Another style of rug commonly found is woven using cotton thread for the warp and strips of cloth, often old used pieces, for the weft; locally this is called KOURELLOUDHES, which translated means tattered cloth. Of course the Handicrafts Centre, mentioned previously, has a whole raft of weavers working together in one room using all these techniques.

The weaver I was most excited to meet however, I discovered by reading an article online in the *Cyprus Mail*. Rolandos Loucaides is a young man with a studio in the Strovolos district of LEFKOSIA. After reading the article I was interested to meet him, as it is unusual to find male weavers in Cyprus these days. In some areas men used heavy looms to weave the heavier thicker cloths, such as the dimity used for VRAKAS and blankets for use under a donkey harness. His studio Odrador also sells his woven materials made into wraps, scarves, handbags, cushions, lavender bags and more. Hanging on the rails were beautifully woven items some with intricate designs in merino wool, alpaca and cotton. Two looms dominated most of the space both set up and in use, one with a piece of FYTHKIOTIKA in progress.

Rolandos studied archaeology originally but became interested in weaving and learned the basic skills at The Handicraft Centre. His main interest, however, is silk weaving as he is fascinated with the patterns produced by the Cypriot silk weavers of the past having studied the remnants of fabrics in museums. But the Handicraft Service could not provide the specialist information he needed to reproduce these patterns and he had to go further afield to Brittany in France, to learn these techniques, which have been used since ancient times in many cultures. After a six-month course he was armed with the necessary information to be able to start decoding those old patterns and start to reproduce them using techniques unused in Cyprus since the 1960s. In silk weaving it is the weaving techniques that make the patterns in the fabric; to be able to appreciate the yarn no additional coloured patterns were considered necessary. This is time consuming and it will take Rolandos time to build up a reputation for such work. As far as we know, he is the only one practicing these techniques in Cyprus and I hope this is the start of a rekindling of interest in these valuable skills.

Right *Rolandos at his loom*

Cypriots are traditionalists and like to do things as they have always been done, which is admirable and has enabled certain traditions to be preserved that otherwise would have been lost. In arts and crafts, however, improvisation and experimentation are also necessary to keep them alive; it allows those crafts to evolve into new and exciting forms, by using knowledge passed down through the generations together with new techniques and innovation. There is a great potential for this in Cyprus with both the basket making and weaving. Therefore I was excited to meet Rolandos, as this is exactly what he is doing: taking the knowledge of ancient techniques using those designs and skills and translating them into his own creations; this is how all the techniques and designs originally came into being, as the weavers experimented to discover what it was possible to create. Rolandos has explored this avenue on his own initiative; the education system has no facility at present to teach traditional techniques and design, with a view to innovation in order to carry the craft forward. What teaching is available is more concerned with preservation. In Britain, however, there is such teaching available and this summer I visited the degree show at Farnham College, UCA, which has a well established and respected textile course both for post and undergraduates. Students come from all over the world, including Cyprus to take advantage of the teaching and well-equipped workshops. We can hope that these students will one day return to Cyprus to enrich the weaving traditions.

Embroidery & Lace

The two centres which have a long history of lace making and are still well known for lace today are OMODHOS and LEVKARA found on the southern slopes of Troodos, both are attractive villages with cobbled streets, which have been restored in recent years. The LEVKARA lace, also known as LEVKARITIKA is known the world over. Merchants took the LEVKARA lace abroad to sell from the mid-19th century, as far afield as the USA and Australia. I have a friend in Britain that remembers his mother getting a visit every year from just such a merchant and her linen cupboard was full to bursting with the purchases that she made over the years.

The methods used to produce LEVKARITIKA are known as drawn and cutwork or drawn thread work. White thread embroidery is usually used on the linen but sometimes a darker brown thread is employed to give contrast. The important feature is the so-called 'river', which consists of a zigzag design that borders the fabric. The designs are mostly geometric, which is dictated by the method employed of counting threads, with occasionally additional embroidery of leaves and flowers. You can tell a good piece of LEVKARITIKA by the stitching, which should be so neat that it is impossible to tell the back from the front. The patterns can be extremely intricate and it has similar characteristics to old Italian embroideries, reflecting the interaction between Venetian and Cypriot civilisations during the Venetian rule of Cyprus in the 16th century. In the past, this technique was used to decorate many parts of the four-poster bed: hangings, sheets, pillowcases and bedcovers. LEVKARA is still known as a centre for this work and it is found in shops wherever you go on the island. There is much machine-made lace around, so if you want to be sure that you are buying the handmade variety go to a reliable source; it is more expensive but of a far superior quality.

Right centre *Old piece of* LEVKARITIKA
Inset left *Cross - stitch*
Inset right KOKKINOPLOUMIA

OMODHOS is famous for the lace work known as PIPILES, which translated means 'narrow-knit laces'. Making knots in the thread using a sewing needle produces this style; it is similar to the method that fishermen use to make nets only on a much, much smaller scale. Intricate, fluid designs can be achieved using this method, which is limited only by the imagination of the lacemaker. OMODHOS has a museum devoted to lace called 'The Centre of the Preservation of Narrow Knit Lace'– not a title that trips off the tongue but leaves you in no doubt as to its function. Housed in one of the old monk's cells adjacent to the monastery it has some fine examples. Its instigators, The Handicraft Services, together with the citizens of OMODHOS, tracked down, studied and recorded the PIPILES lace. Don't be afraid to ask if you find it closed, as usually someone will be happy to open the museum for you to visit.

OMODHOS has many shops selling lace of all descriptions and if you are looking particularly for something handmade the shopkeepers are very willing to show you authentic pieces. There is a very good shop directly opposite the side entrance to the monastery on the corner where I purchased a beautiful table runner of ASPROPLOUMIA, which I turned into a cover for the back of a dining chair. Now I can sit and admire it hanging down with its beautiful fringe made of twists of crochet. ASPROPLOUMIA, translated means simply white embroidery. It is a popular style on the island and is executed on a white cotton cloth with wide blocks and borders of a design either made with a needle or crocheted, with parts of drawn thread work. These pieces can make very attractive curtains and traditionally this type of work covered the glass in the doors and windows, as well as used to line shelves with the border hanging over the edge acting as a fringe. Other traditional styles of embroidery are cross-stitch, which is found all over the world and,

in particular, KOKKINOPLOUMIA, which translated means 'red embroidery' and uses only red thread. TSEVREDES uses brightly coloured silks on a linen or silk background and generally employs running and darning stitches. Unlike other types of embroidery TSEVREDES uses more floral designs and motifs. Many old examples show beautifully fine work. All these techniques were once used to decorate everyday objects and clothing, turning the mundane

Left & Right
ASPROPLOUMIA
examples

into a thing of beauty. Women were liberated from this kind of everyday occupation when opportunities to join the modern world of work and availability of manufactured and imported goods meant this was no longer possible or necessary. Those who care to use them, to make works of art to be admired and cherished in a different setting, have now adopted these skills. Encouragingly as recently as April 2011, an exhibition of contemporary costume design was held in Levkara, the result of collaboration between lacemakers of Levkara and some craftworkers from Slovakia, Croatia and Britain. This event was organised by The Green Villages project, which is an initiative bringing together nine European countries with similar problems of migration from rural areas, which work together with the aid of education to help bring new life and sustainable development to the rural communities.

Pottery & Ceramics

Pottery has been around since prehistoric times. The early terracotta pots found in Cyprus were made from the local clay, which is used still today to make unglazed and glazed pots. The main centres known for pottery were KORNOS, FOINI, LAPITHOS and VAROSHA. White clay from the VAROSHA area was used to make sewer pipes and unglazed water vessels among other things. The cooling facility of an unglazed pot has a magical simplicity: the porous pot keeps the water cool inside the water vessel by the constant evaporation of the water on the outside. A decorative style used to adorn pots, which is typical of this area, is to apply models of animals, birds, flowers and people to the outside and has resulted in some

Left Pottery of George Georgiadhes

fantastical looking objects involving a whole array of figures. Examples of these can be viewed in museums but this style is still replicated today in areas such as FOINI and KORNOS.

Until Hellenistic times the artistic culture of Cyprus flourished, the potters of Cyprus developed a rich and diverse range of pottery but then followed many years of turbulence when the island was plundered by invaders and tyrants. For centuries, as the islanders struggled to survive, the artistic culture dwindled. The original method of processing clay, which later became mechanised, involved digging it out of the ground and allowing it to dry before pulverising it with a wooden pole, then sieving to remove unwanted pebbles and debris. When the potter wishes to prepare the clay for potting, water is sprinkled over it and allowed to soak in before the clay is mixed with a wooden paddle. The wheel, used to turn the smaller items, sits on the ground and the potter sits on a low stool to work it, turning the wheel with their feet or legs. Pottery was very much a cottage industry and women were engaged in the making of the smaller objects while the men did the heavy work and made the larger pots. The huge PITHARI were made using the coil technique taking about 30 days to complete; the clay was kept damp by laying walnut or vine leaves over the surface at the end of each day. Then they were left to dry for 10 days before being fired in a wood fired kiln for three days. PITHARI were used for all kinds

Left (top & bottom) Pots at Mr. Pilivakes Museum, (centre) Traditional pot made at The Handicraft centre

Left Some of the PITHARI in Mr Pilivakes' museum

of storage including wine, vinegar and oil, and were made waterproof by spreading the interior with hot tar made out of pine resin. FOINI became known predominantly for making PITHARI and pottery generally brought the village prosperity, so much so that the neighbouring villages of KAMINARIA and AYIOS DEMETRIOS decided to follow their example. The potters of FOINI were known to be itinerant and would make camp near the wine-making villages, often bringing their clay with them to make the PITHARI on the spot, this ruled out the dangers of damage in transit.

On our visit to KAMINARIA, Androula sought out Avghi, who she had been told was a traditional potter. In the usual manner with nothing to go by except the fact that she lived in KAMINARIA, she enquired at various houses until we found her house up a steep side road. Avghi has one of those beautiful faces, worn with age but still sparkling with energy and a hint of mischief in her eyes. She welcomed us warmly as she invited us to pass through her yard into her kitchen, which was located in a separate building in the traditional village manner. Utilitarian and spotlessly clean with a tiled floor and white plastered walls fitted out with modern kitchen units, shelves crammed full of china, family photographs and icons spilling across the spare surfaces, we were invited to sit and offered refreshments. Avghi told us that many years ago a US university came to make a film of her at work, as she is one of the few remaining traditional potters. Showing us some small examples of her work, incense burners that she had made when demonstrating, she made a gift of them to us. Had she known we were coming, she told us, she would have given us a demonstration, which was alas another sacrifice of my limited time. As it was we made do with seeing the wheel she uses, the dry clay and the finished articles she had made a lot earlier.

Right Avghi and her wheel

Left Incense burners

The mechanics of the making we would just have to imagine. After making our farewells we walked back through KAMINARIA and I noticed a derelict circular stone built kiln by the side of the road. There is another similar brick kiln in AYIOS DIMITRIOS, which has been restored. These were once used communally by the villagers to fire their pots but, alas, no longer.

In FOINI Mr Pilavakis has set up a museum, which houses some fine examples of the pots his family has made over many generations, and he kindly gave me a brief tour when I visited. Passing through the ancient, weather beaten doors from the road, I found myself in a shady pleasant yard filled with the paraphernalia of a bygone age together with all manner and sizes of pots. Dotted around the periphery of the yard were stone grinding mills used for olive pressing and a wine press with its huge wooden corkscrew. The last PITHARI made here was in 1972 and he informed me they are not made anywhere on the island today. Mr Pilavakis told me of an unusual use for the very large PITHARI and one of which I had not heard before; it was utilised as a sauna for women after giving birth to help them get back into shape. A charcoal fire would be lit in the pot and 5 litres of water with herbs set to boil and produce steam. The woman would sit for an hour in the steam on a low chair with the hole of the pot covered and leaving just a small space for the woman to breathe; a bit like an early version of a

steam cabinet. She would then undergo a massage and this would be repeated twice a week for a month when, he reliably informed me, she would have recovered her beautiful figure.

The pottery from LAPITHOS had a distinctive band of green glaze around the top, and Androula has collected several of these early pots over the years. In the early 20th century there was an influx of Greek refugees from Asia Minor who settled here and with them they brought new techniques and shapes, which enriched the pottery styles. I have a set of delicate coffee cups decorated with trailing vine leaves, which my mother bought for me on a visit there many years ago and they bring back fond memories of

this beautiful place with its rippling stream close by and dappled shade. This area is now under Turkish occupation and the potters displaced. Androula also has some contemporary pottery, which I admired on a previous visit, that was made by her potter friend George Georgiadhes at LEMBA Pottery. I wanted to pay him a visit and, after ringing ahead to make an appointment, I set forth to find him.

George and his wife Sotiroula have a studio and shop in LEMBA, which is known to be an artist's village, slightly off the beaten track but well worth a visit. The simple, elegant lines of his pottery, which is contemporary in its execution, has echoes of his cultural past, which has inevitably influenced him.

The glazes are mellow and earthy with some vibrant blues and greens reminiscent of the Mediterranean sea and sky. George studied not only his father's techniques, a potter in LAPITHOS, but also read of others' techniques, developing his own style. His studio, a world away from Avghi's simple yard, has racks of pots lined up ready for firing, thrown on a modern electric wheel. George uses stoneware clays from Britain and Germany that, when fired at high temperatures, in his huge gas kiln, gives a durable finish, unlike the traditional local clay which chips easily. His work is only available in his shop, as he doesn't supply any other outlets.

We had an interesting chat about the status of the craft of pottery in Cyprus today. He told me that although there are opportunities to exhibit abroad and funding is available it isn't always easy to access the information via the official channels. He finds there is some lack of communication and indeed willingness to get the information broadcast to as many ceramicists and potters as possible. George is a member of the Cyprus Pottery-Ceramic Association along with 39 other potters and ceramicists, many of whom have studied abroad and brought their knowledge and experience back to Cyprus to set up small studios around the island.

Another member of the association is Koula Kalvari who owns the ceramics studio Keramidea. I dropped in to see her when I was in LEFKOSIA, her studio and

shop is housed in one of the attractive old buildings within the city walls near The Famagusta Gate. Her work covers three areas, jewelry, applied work on small ceramics, such as bowls and mugs, and purely expressive works of art using ceramics, material and string. I found some of her work very emotive and powerful as well as decorative. I came away with a simple ceramic kite, which hangs on a wall near my landing window, its string tail, decorated with scraps of material catches in the breeze when the window is open. Koula has exhibited in Cairo and Greece as well as successfully securing a place in the Malta–Cyprus Ceramics Exhibition in 2007/8. This exhibition is run every two years alternating between Malta and Cyprus and features works from selected Cypriot and Maltese ceramicists allowing a cultural exchange of ideas.

Art

During my conversation with George he recommended that I visit Lemba College of Art, which was just up the road. As I turned the corner and caught site of the wall outside the college I was very glad I had taken the trouble to see it and a smile spread across my face. The wall, which is 20m long and up to 4m high in places, is a celebration, a festival, and a positive riot of sculptural styles all blending into one another to produce a unique and vibrant unity. Started in 1992 by the founder of the college Stass Paraskos it includes found and recycled everyday objects. As I walked through the gates the festival continued its exuberance into the courtyard.

Sadly the facilities inside the college are much more down-to-earth and are no more than a group of connecting rooms with leaky roofs. Luckily the weather is amenable so much of the work is done outside. The annual summer studio offers the students a space to work with tutors and, for a limited time, take advantage of their help and advice. Stass Paraskos founded The Cyprus College of Art in 1969. A Cypriot artist, he trained in Britain and enjoyed a teaching career, which culminated at the Kent Institute of Art and Design where he became a senior lecturer in Fine Art as well as Head of Painting. He has exhibited all over the world and Tate Britain houses one of his paintings. Originally based in AMMOCHOSTOS (Famagusta) the college came to rest in LEMBA after the 1974 Turkish Invasion forced them to flee. Since 2007 its main campus has been in LARNAKA where it is housed in a traditional townhouse. The College offers courses up to M.A. level including a very popular postgraduate diploma course. The students in the past have been from outside Cyprus but from 2000 the college has been encouraging Cypriot students to apply.

When I think of Cyprus it conjures up many things to me: it is a country with layers of richness – historical, cultural, topographical and gastronomical. This is a country with a long and complicated history and it has an enormous wealth of ancient artifacts, including many beautiful frescoes and icons. Ecclesiastical iconographers were always present

of course and religious works were being produced continually. But what always puzzled me was the lack of evidence of any developing art culture outside of the church between ancient and modern times. While researching this book I have come to realise that the struggle and upheaval of the Cypriot people has meant that, until very recently, there has been little time for artistic exploration. As already discussed, the areas where an artistic temperament could be expressed was in the production of everyday items, such as basket making, weaving or pottery. Education until the 1830s was mainly under the authority of priests. After 1453 Cypriots travelled abroad, Constantinople, Alexandria, Venice, Paris or Rome to gain higher education. This became an established tradition, especially after the founding of The University of Athens in 1937. And this continues today with approximately 30 to 40 per cent of Cypriot students going to Greece to study for their degrees. Only for the past 30 years has Cyprus had its own universities and colleges but they are growing all the time.

There must have always been some naive painters but the considered father of contemporary Cypriot naive art was Michael Kashalos born in 1885 in the village of ASSIA. He was self-taught and started his career by painting on glass, which was fashionable in villages in the early 1900s. A shoemaker by trade he didn't start painting until 1957. A contemporary of Kashalos was Admantios Diamantis born in 1900 he went to

London to study at The Royal College of Art, returning to his native land after a couple of years to teach and paint studies of the local villagers whom he observed; often from his vantage point in the coffee shop no doubt. He experimented with various styles and his work had an important influence on later Cypriot artists. Works from both of these artists can be found in The State Gallery of Contemporary Cypriot Art in LEFKOSIA.

I have been excited to find evidence of an expanding interest and appreciation of contemporary art over the past few years. One great example is The Municipal Art Centre of LEFKOSIA, which is housed in the Old Electric House. The Cyprus Electricity Authority donated the building, which was derelict for 20 years, to the Nicosia Municipality and it is the best example of Cypriot industrial architecture. Built in the 1920s, using the fundamental rules of the Bauhaus movement of functional simplified design, it was the first electric power station in LEFKOSIA. It has been carefully restored and converted into a very modern art gallery, leaving as much of the original structure intact as possible, including the original gantry of the old power station. The gallery opened in 1994 and was the first project of the municipality's scheme to regenerate the area close to the Green line that divides the Greek and the Turkish occupied parts of LEFKOSIA. There has been a close collaboration with Dimitris Pierides Museum Of Contemporary Art in Athens and The Modern Greek Engravings

Left The Old Electric House gallery LEFKOSIA

Collection, has been loaned by them for exhibition. Mr Pierides has also donated a large collection of art history books and art magazines to the museum, which has created a reference library and a unique resource for the city.

There are three permanent exhibitions, as well as a changing programme of exhibitions involving collaborations with museums and foundations around the world. The aim of the museum is to encourage and promote contemporary art in Cyprus and, of course, exhibits works by Cypriot and Greek artists. As with all good museums and galleries it also has a restaurant. I was fortunate enough to pay a visit while a Miro exhibition was showing and I was duly impressed with both the space and the sensitivity with which the building has been treated, I could see why it had been awarded a Europa Nostra Award on completion.

REVITALISED LEFKOSIA

In this area of LEFKOSIA there is a great deal of restoration work being carried out on many of the old buildings, giving the neighbourhood a fresh vibrancy, the finished buildings painted in pastel shades with pedestrianised areas. Many artists are attracted to this quarter and at the CHRYSALINIOTISSA Craft centre there are eight workshops around a central courtyard housing various artisans including a carver, an icon painter and a glass studio.

Next to these is Inga's Veggie Heaven. The café is on the site of a previous well-loved and long-standing café, which used to serve traditional vegetable-based dishes beloved of the older generation of workers. It now serves a different kind of vegetarian dish. All the food is freshly made each day, including their own bread, and all are packed with flavour. We stopped for rest and refreshments after our visit to the

Above Icon painter
Chrysaliniotissa centre

Above Inga's Veggie Heaven

art centre and I had a savoury SPANOKOPITTA, (a spinach and cheese pie), while my niece and nephew had a sugar-free cake. It all smelled delicious as indeed it tasted. Inga Hadjipanayi is from Iceland, married to a Cypriot and is passionate about organic, vegetarian food, lending a new twist to some familiar traditional favourites.

In present-day Cyprus more than ever there are people of all nationalities not only passing through but also settling here. Joining the EU has brought many Eastern Europeans seeking work, also second generation Cypriots born abroad in Australia, USA and Britain have come to live and work here. All these elements inevitably bring a more cosmopolitan feel to the country as well as an extra dimension to the cuisine. Fundamentally the Cypriot identity remains intact. In the next section we will explore the rich diversity of traditional Cypriot cuisine and some of its origins.

Left Revitalised LEFKOSIA

Right LEFKOSIA

Food
Glorious
Food

Food Culture
of Cyprus

Cypriots and food is a loving pair. Cyprus is a fertile country with a temperate climate all year round so almost anything can be grown here. Over the centuries the richness of the land, together with its abundance of copper and silver, brought many traders and settlers to her shores; one of the very earliest being the Ancient Greeks. It also brought a constant succession of invaders and rulers: Egyptian, Persian, Byzantine, Greek, Roman, Arab, Crusader, Lusignan, Venetian, Turkish and British until Cyprus finally became independent in 1960. Although the Greek culture prevails throughout, the food of Cyprus naturally reflects the many cultures that have passed through the island over the years.

The people of Cyprus make full use of the abundant produce and have a varied diet, which includes a vast array of seasonal fruit and vegetables. Agriculture no longer plays such a large role in the Cypriot economy but there are more than 30 fresh produce exporters, at the time of writing, including fresh herbs, which are a growth area for the country. Vines, potatoes and citrus fruits are the backbone of food production these days and methods of farming are increasingly being mechanised and modernised. Organic production of some foods is increasing, and you can now buy organic wines, olive oils, salt and in 2004 an organic dairy farm, Riverland, was set up. It supplies organic dairy products from its goats as well as meat. In these more prosperous times, meat features largely in most Cypriots' diets but in the past the villagers kept pigeons, rabbits, chickens, pigs and goats for their meat and so it was eaten more sparingly. Chicken is the universal ever-adaptable staple and in Cyprus it is most commonly boiled, yielding a flavourful stock that is used not only for making: AVGOLEMONO soup and the cooking of TRAHANA but also the RAVIOLES and MACARONIA, that together with the chicken meat sprinkled generously with grated HALLOUMI, is eaten for Saturday lunch. Chicken is also frequently cooked with COLOCASSI or cooked in wine in a KRASATO dish or simply jointed and roasted in the oven with potatoes.

Traditionally village families would buy a pig in September at the PANAGYRI (religious festival) and

Right Goatherd in FYTI

fatten it up for Christmas when they would make AFELIA, SOUVLAKIA and COLOCASSI and so on with the fresh meat. There are many dishes which use pork either cubed or minced, as you will read in some of the following recipes, it is still the most commonly eaten meat after chicken. The rest of the meat was preserved by making delicacies such as LOUKANIKA, very spicy sausages, CHOIROMERI a smoked, spiced ham, LOUNZA smoked pork loin and ZALATINA, a brawn.

Red wine is used in the preserving of many of the meat products as it was, and still is, readily available, made from the prolific vines growing in the surrounding areas. In the villages every house had a couple of goats, which were kept for their milk and at Easter one young goat would be eaten at the celebration meal, the rest sold for income. The milk would be used to make ANARI, HALLOUMI and yoghurt as well as TRAHANA. The women of the village, who were responsible for the cheese making, would club together to form a co-operative to pool their milk. Once a fortnight they would take it in turns to keep it and keep a tally of how much milk each woman provided. When there was enough the cheese making would begin and shared out when finished. Cheese was only made for a few months of the year while the milk was being produced, so it was kept in containers filled with brine and mint to preserve it. The older the cheese the harder and saltier it becomes.

Meze

When eating out in Cyprus the menu will invariably mention MEZEDHES or MEZE and serves a similar purpose to Spanish tapas in providing many small dishes of appetizers. It includes a wide variety of foods, and can be eaten as the accompaniment to a drink or as a full-blown meal. When visiting a Cypriot house it is customary for the guest to be offered a drink of coffee, wine or brandy, accompanied by a choice of several little tit-bits to nibble: either nuts or pieces of fruit, olives, SOUSHOUKO, maybe some LOUKANIKA or grilled HALLOUMI, whatever is available. As a child whenever we had visitors, my dad would always cut up an apple, orange or perhaps celery, as well as offering nuts and crisps. I used to think this was a very nice idea.

MEZE is a great choice if a large group is dining out as it means you can try out all the dishes and decide which are your favourites. Be warned, MEZE can be a mammoth affair, so make sure you all have a good appetite or you could be going home with several days worth of leftovers.

MEZE generally start with dips such as:

TAHINOSALATA Tahini (ground sesame seeds) mixed with quantities of garlic and lemon juice

TARAMOSALATA A fish-roe dip made with the salty cured cod or carp fish roe.

TALATTOURI Also known as TZATZIKI, which is its Turkish name, this dip is made with yoghurt, mint, garlic and cucumber, and a little salt.

SKORDHALIA This is made with macerated bread, and occasionally cooked potato, as well as several cloves of garlic, olive oil, lemon juice and salt to taste. It is usually eaten as an accompaniment to BAKALIAROS (salt cod), among other things.

MELITZANOSALATA Cooked aubergine flesh mashed with tahini, garlic, lemon juice and salt.

MELITZANOSALADA

This is a puree made with the smoked flesh of aubergine and tahini and has a strong garlic flavour. It is served with toasted PITTA bread or chunks of fresh bread for dipping.

Here is a recipe that Androula gave me.

Serves 4–6
2 large aubergines
2 tablespoons tahini
3 cloves garlic
2 teaspoons lemon juice
2 teaspoons olive oil
Pinch of salt

Wash and dry the aubergines. To prevent them bursting while cooking, pierce each one with a fork at the ends. Place under the grill for about 30 to 40 minutes, regularly turning them to cook on all sides until the skins are burned and blistered and they are cooked through. Alternatively the aubergines can be baked in the oven and the skins blistered over a flame afterwards if you prefer. It is the blackened skin that gives the dip its smoked flavour. When the inside is soft and cooked, cut them lengthwise and remove the pulp. Crush the garlic with a little salt to make into a paste and mash together the pulp, and tahini. Add lemon juice and olive oil in equal quantities and mix well together. Adjust to taste.

After the dips comes a succession of vegetable dishes, fish and meat and always a dish of the local small green olives, ELIES TSAKISSTES. These have been cracked and soaked in water until the bitterness has gone, then marinated in oil with garlic and coriander seeds. Among the many dishes you will find some of the ones mentioned in the following pages, KEFTEDHES, KOUPEPIA, STIFADO, KLEFTICO, TAVAS and so on and on and on … each taverna has their own specialities.

Accompanying any meal, and MEZE is no exception, there is always a village salad as it is commonly called in Cyprus also known as a Greek salad. This again will vary according to the taverna and season but these are the basic ingredients in order of preparation and are often layered finishing off with the crumbled feta.

VILLAGE SALAD

Simply combine finely shredded white cabbage, cubed cucumber, quartered tomatoes and finely sliced onions or spring onions. Scatter with olives and crumbled feta cheese then dress with olive oil and lemon juice and season with salt and pepper before serving.

At the end of the banquet a very welcome dish of KARPOUZI (watermelon) is served and washed down with a coffee and brandy, Cypriot of course and possibly some LOUKOUMIA.

HALLOUMI

HALLOUMI is the most universal of the cheeses made on the island and the by-product is ANARI, which is made from the whey, forming a soft mild cheese similar to ricotta. HALLOUMI is a unique cheese because it doesn't separate when heated and cooked. Androula's friend Rosie talked me through the process of making HALLOUMI.

Goat's or sheep's milk can be used for making HALLOUMI but sheep's is better as it has a milder flavour. The unpasteurised milk is strained through muslin into a container and heated to about 30C or just below scalding point. Then the heat is turned off and a small amount of rennet is added. It is left

for about 30 minutes, until the milk has turned to yoghurt, and then broken up either by running your fingers through it or cutting it into small cubes. Then is placed over the heat again to warm. As it warms up the curds are collected with a slotted spoon and put aside to drain and any remaining water squeezed out. The remaining liquid is heated again and brought to a higher temperature to make it separate once more producing smaller lumps, which are collected and put to drain in a TALARI. These can be eaten warm with sugar or carob syrup, which is delicious, or used to make ANARI. The ANARI can be eaten fresh or salt can be added, which preserves it. The curds are shaped and put back into the cooking liquid, and heated to cook the cheese for another 30 minutes. When the cheese rises to the surface it is ready.

It can be eaten fresh or preserved with salt crystals and mint, folded over and stored in brine. The brine is made up from the liquid remaining in the pot. Alternatively, this liquid can be used to cook a chicken and then used as broth or stock.

As well as feta, which is usually crumbled on top of the ubiquitous village salads, the other cheeses produced in Cyprus are KEFALOTIRI, a hard yellow cheese made from sheep or ewe's milk with a salty, nutty flavour similar to Gruyere and KASKAVALO another yellow cheese with holes similar to the Italian *Caciocavallo*, which was probably introduced to Cyprus by the Italians at the time of Venetian rule.

TSAMARELLA

Goat meat is preserved by making it into TSAMARELLA: either goat or sheep can be preserved in this way and the shepherds used to know salty stones in the fields where they would leave the meat to dry while tending their flocks.

First the meat is de-boned and cut into large sections then deep cuts are made three-quarters of the way through the flesh. Salt is well rubbed into these cuts and then the meat is rolled up and left in a bowl or tray to drain until the next day. The next day the meat is unrolled and the excess salt washed off. The meat is then suspended, covered with mesh to protect it, and left in the sun and turned every day until it is dry. The meat is then taken piece by piece and put in boiling water for a minute each, washed in cold water, then tenderised by pounding it a little with a mallet. It is left again until it is dry and then can either be hung or kept in the fridge.

LOUKANIKA

The meat from the front shoulder and leg of the pig, as well as some bacon is used to make LOUKANIKA. The meat is cut into very small pieces, or better still coarsely ground in a meat grinder before being put in a bowl with some salt, covered in red wine and left for two days, all the while being checked to ensure the meat is always covered with wine. After two days, it is stirred and cinnamon, pepper and finely chopped red peppers are added, together with crushed coriander seeds and a few crushed cloves and SCHINUS berries. The ingredients are mixed well together and stuffed into its casing of pigs intestines to make sausages.

Right CHEIROMERI in Elpiniki's kitchen

Left The lovely Irinoula who runs the coffee shop in KAMINARIA and a renowned cook locally, was very generous with her time when Androula and I visited her. She supplied the above information regarding preserving meats.

ZALATINA

This one you can try at home, it's a recipe for making brawn!

Take the whole head of a pig and cut out the mouth and snout. Put the head together with the trotters in enough water to cover them with some salt and lemon juice. When it comes to the boil drain the contents and throw the water away. Wash the head and trotters well with clean water. Put them again in clean water to boil with salt and lemon juice, skimming off any scum that rises to the surface. When the meat is cooked remove from the water, reserving the cooking liquid put the meat in a bowl to leave overnight. The next day remove the fat and discard. Cut all the meat from the bones, cutting into small pieces as you prefer and place in a casserole dish. At this stage other cooked meat, from the shoulder, can be added. Remove any fat sitting on top of the stock and add 284ml of lemon juice, 284ml of bitter orange juice, 568ml of vinegar and a sprig or two of rosemary to the remainder. Heat the jellied stock until it has turned to liquid and adjust to taste. Remove from the heat, take out the rosemary and allow to cool a little before pouring over the meat in the casserole. Leave it to cool before putting it in the fridge to set.

CHOIROMERI

Elpiniki of KAMINARIA gave us a rough outline of how CHIROMERI is produced traditionally. The haunch of a pig is covered in a lot of salt and placed in a tray with the thick end facing down resting against a log and left to drain (the log is surrounded by the haunches). The juices are removed every day for three days, the tray is cleaned and the meat replaced with more salt and left to drain. During this time, it is important that the air is allowed to circulate around the meat. The meat is then put in a container, covered in red wine and left for 20 days. It is then pressed to remove as much juice as possible. The meat is then smoked over a fire three or four times, pressed in-between times to extract more juice. This is a time-consuming and difficult process and so the resulting delicacy is appreciated all the more.

SEASONINGS & SPICES

In Cypriot cooking there are several spices, which are used frequently. Many, such as cinnamon, which is used in both savoury and sweet things, cumin, oregano and coriander, are universally known while others are more unusual such as:

MECHLEPI is the crushed kernel of a cherry.

MASTICHA comes from the mastic tree (Pistacia Lentiscus) also known as the Schinos tree. The resin from the bark is used for many purposes, including as a seasoning and chewing gum. MASTICHA comes from the Greek word to 'chew'. Once collected, the resin is sold as small crystals or beads, which are crushed before used to flavour foods. Mastic trees grow on Cyprus but the seasoning comes from the trees grown on the Greek island of Chios, however, the berries, a kind of pink peppercorn, can be used as a seasoning in LOUKANIKA.

MAVROKOKKOS are tiny black seeds of nigella sativa but black onion seeds are also referred to as MAVROKOKKOS in some places and used on breads and rusks.

TREMITHIA (Terebinth – Pistacia Terebinthus) a small tree that produces berries a little bigger than a whole black peppercorn and are used as a seasoning.

On my fact-finding trip to Cyprus I wanted to gather recipes from the people I met and Androula had the great idea to invite our Aunt Eugenia to come and stay at TREIS ELIES to show us the many recipes she made using wheat, and which my grandmother used to make. Granny lived with Aunt Eugenia in the village until she died and Androula lived next door when she was a child. She fondly remembered how the children would cluster around Granny when she cooked sweet things eagerly waiting for a taste, so we looked forward to doing the same when Auntie came to stay.

I collected my Aunt from LEFKOSIA and we journeyed together on a sizzlingly hot day in May up the many winding roads of Troodos to TREIS ELIES. Stopping only to gaze at the frescoes at PANAGIA FORVIOTISSA TIS ASINOU on the way. We arrived very hot and tired and after climbing the steep, steps up to Androula's terrace we sat in the shady cool and partook of some welcome refreshment. Staying with Androula for the beginning of our visit was a friend, Rosie, who had lived in London for some years and spoke very good English, which was a great help in translating some of the information that came up that first evening as we dived straight in to the cooking.

Soups

The first thing Androula wanted to tell me about was the soups that are commonly cooked. The simplest of these, and the most humble, is LOUVANA. IT uses a very small amount of ingredients but makes a very tasty soup. The recipe varies from village to village but it always contains split peas and rice. Generally the soup is thick and creamy as a result of the split peas breaking down during cooking.

LOUVANA

This is a good warming soup for the winter and if you like you can add a little chilli but hot spices are used less frequently in Cyprus these days. Traditionally this soup is eaten on Good Friday, as the vinegar serves as a reminder of when Jesus was offered vinegar to drink on the cross.

This is the recipe Androula's mother used.

Serves 4

1 litre water
1 carrot, finely sliced
1 small onion or a leek or spring onions, finely sliced
1 stick of celery, finely sliced
1 potato, finely cubed
200g LOUVANA (yellow split peas)
200g long grain rice

Put the water to boil in a large pan. Add the vegetables, potato, split peas and rice to the boiling water. Turn down the heat and allow to simmer gently and stirring from time to time to prevent sticking to the bottom of the pan, until the split peas and rice are cooked and the vegetables are tender. Season with salt and pepper to taste.

Serve with a few drops of olive oil and a dash of vinegar or bitter orange. A little squeezed lemon juice can also be added if you like.

My Aunt told us that when times were very hard, the villagers would make a very simple soup by cooking some POURGOURRI (cracked wheat) in water and then sprinkling the soup with small pieces of fried bread.

AVGOLEMONO

This is another simple soup, which is very traditional and eaten on high days and holidays. Translated AVGOLEMONO means eggs and lemon.

Serves 4–5
1 litre fresh home-made chicken stock
160g risotto rice
2 medium eggs
Juice of 2 lemons
Salt and pepper

Cook the rice in the stock, homemade is preferable. While this is cooking, whisk the eggs and lemon juice together in a separate bowl until frothy. When the rice is cooked, about 12 minutes, remove from the heat, and to prevent curdling, slowly add the stock to the lemon and egg mixture a tablespoon at a time, stirring all the time. When all the ingredients are added together return the pan to the heat and heat through gently but do not let it boil or the eggs will cook. Season with salt and pepper to taste and serve immediately.

ENTRADA SOUP

This is another recipe from Rosie, which makes a good hearty meal.

Serves 6–8
1 kilo lamb chops
1 kilo potatoes, cubed
1 onion, chopped
Handful of parsley, chopped
3 eggs
1 lemon
Salt and pepper to taste

Boil the lamb in enough water to cover the meat well, skimming off any scum that rises to the surface. When the lamb is cooked add the potatoes, onion and parsley. When the potatoes are soft remove from the heat. Beat the eggs with the juice of the lemon in a separate bowl and, using the same technique as the AVGOLEMONO soup, add a little of the broth, a spoonful at a time to the egg and lemon mixture. Then add this lemon and egg mixture to the ENTRADA and warm through gently to serve. Season with salt and pepper to taste.

TRAHANA

TRAHANA soup is very dear to most Cypriots' hearts. Again this is eaten on high days and holidays, and my dad remembered it fondly. It is, however, an acquired taste as the TRAHANA is made with sour goats milk and wheat, which is then dried and stored for later use.

Ascetic and sour notes are threaded throughout Cypriot food.

The milk used to make TRAHANA is prepared by adding a little salt to it, and then leaving it in a covered unglazed earthenware jar in a cool place for 10 to 15 days. Every three days it is stirred and more milk added until you have the required amount of milk and the fermentation is complete.

The wheat is washed and crushed between two stones, the same as in the preparation of POURGOURI. Using the ratio of 3 litres of the soured milk to 1 kilo of crushed wheat, the milk is put in a large cauldron and brought to the boil and then the wheat is gradually added. It is stirred continuously until it has the consistency of thick gruel when it is ready to take off the heat and left to cool. Once cooled it is either cut into slices or made into small nuggets and left to dry in the sun on a TSESTOS. The TRAHANA is stored in jars or sacks hung from the ceiling and kept for use in the winter. This is still made at home in some rural areas usually during August and September but is also mass produced and readily available in supermarkets. Even if mass-produced, this product has no additives or preservatives and is a highly nutritious food.

TRAHANA SOUP

This is Rosie's recipe and is extremely simple to make.

Serves 6
200g TRAHANA to 1½ litres home-made chicken stock

The TRAHANA is put in a bowl with a little water and left until it becomes soft, like cooked rice. Bring the stock to boil, add the softened TRAHANA and put in a little bit of chopped celery, carrot and a whole chopped onion. Lower the heat and gently simmer until the vegetables are cooked. When the vegetables are cooked the soup is ready, add some small cubes of HALLOUMI and serve. To add even more of a sour bite, a little yoghurt can be added at the table. Season with salt and pepper to taste.

***Right** Chicken, homemade pasta and bread eaten with grated HALLOUMI & yoghurt*

Wheat

Wheat was used in a multitude of ways and played a very important role in everyday meals, as did pulses or OSPRIA. When Androula was planning the recipes that she wanted Aunt Eugenia to show us, she came to realize how much the Cypriots traditionally relied on wheat. It was the most widely grown grain and its uses in cooking are wide and varied. We have already covered TRAHANA, and another wheat product frequently used is POURGOURI, known as bulgur wheat. It is made by cooking the wheat grains in water then leaving them to dry in the sun, either on a TSESTOS or a clean cloth. In Cyprus it was sometimes left on the roof to dry if there was no space elsewhere. When dry it is ground between two stones.

POURGOURI PILAFI

This is one of my favourite recipes, eaten with some fresh sheep's yoghurt and a side salad. It is a dish in itself, although it is generally eaten as an accompaniment to AFELIA.

Serves 4 as a side dish
1 tablespoons of olive oil
1dessertspoon PHIDHE (orzo pasta) or vermicelli
1 medium onion, finely chopped
1 dessertspoon tomato paste or tomato puree or 1
beefsteak tomato, grated
200g POURGOURI
568ml water
Salt to taste

Heat the oil in the pan and cook the PHIDHE or vermicelli until browned but not burned. Add the onion and cook until soft then add the grated beefsteak tomato and cook for a few minutes until soft also. Season with salt to taste.

Add the POURGOURI, and mix well then the water and stir again. If you're using tomato paste or puree, instead of fresh tomato, dilute them with a little of the water before adding to the POURGOURRI. Bring to the boil on a high heat then cover and reduce the heat to simmer. Cook for 10 minutes. Turn off the heat and, without removing the lid, leave for a further 5 minutes until the POURGOURRI is plump and all the moisture absorbed.

BREAD

The most universal product made from wheat is bread. In Cyprus there are certain foods that are eaten at specific times of the year and connected to religious observance; some dishes are eaten at times of fasting, others when fasting is over. Bread is such an important staple of the diet that there are, of course, particular types, which are baked only for specific religious occasions.

ARTOS is the ancient Greek word for bread and is the word used for all the breads used in religious observance.

PROSPHORON is the bread that is taken at Holy Communion.

PANISIDA is a large loaf covered in sesame seeds offered at the church on special memorial and celebrations days and then shared among the congregation.

TSOUREKI is sweet plaited Easter bread made with milk and eggs, which is more a Greek custom but is now eaten in Cyprus.

The other treat available at Easter is FLAOUNES, a real favourite of mine, which are individual open pies filled with a delicious mixture of eggs, mint and a goat's milk cheese made especially for this purpose.

The recipe for basic bread dough is fairly universal, but my Aunt Eugenia makes her bread with half plain white flour and half wholemeal flour. She doesn't measure out quantities as she cooks by eye. She also makes her own starter, which results in a sourdough bread. For simplicity this recipe uses dried yeast.

BASIC BREAD RECIPE

225g white bread flour
225g wholemeal bread flour
1 teaspoon salt
1 teaspoon sugar
1 heaped teaspoon quick yeast
¼ teaspoon MASTICHA
¼ teaspoon MECHLEPI
284ml tepid water
1 tablespoon olive oil

Topping
1 teaspoon aniseed
1 teaspoon MAVROKOKKOS
1 teaspoon sesame seeds (optional)

Put the flour in a bowl together with the salt, sugar, quick yeast, MASTICHA and MECHLEPI. Make a well in the centre and pour in the tepid water. Bring the flour into the centre and pull together then add the olive oil and continue to pull together, using your hands to mix and knead until all the ingredients are incorporated.

Knead the dough well on a board, by pushing the dough away from you with the heel of your hand then folding it over quarter turning it and repeating the process for at least 10 minutes, or until the dough is smooth and elastic. Shape into a ball and put on a floured baking sheet, sprinkle with a mixture of either aniseed and MAVROKOKKOS or poppy seeds (you can add sesame seeds, too, if you like them). Cover with a cloth and leave to rise in a warm, draught-free place until doubled in size, this should take about an hour.

Preheat the oven to gas mark 8 /225C. Before putting in the oven score a circular mark around the top with a knife. Cook in the very hot oven for 10 minutes then reduce down to 200C/gas mark 6 for about 25 to 35 minutes or until golden brown. The bread should sound hollow when tapped. Leave to cool.

There is a range of traditional wooden boards used in the making of bread, although some of them have been replaced by plastic versions. The traditional board is called a SKAFI and is a trough-like container made of wood in which you can make and knead the bread.

A long narrow board with hollows along its length where the loaves rest while they are rising is called PINAKOTI or KOUPOSSANIO and a traditional pastry board is a DKIARTOSANIO.

Right Androula took me to
visit a woman in OMODHOS
that is famous for making
these ARKATENA
KOLOURIA She uses the
traditional clay oven to cook
them and they are so popular
that every day she sells all
she can make. Loaves can be
made using this dough but
she is famous for making the
hard rusk type, which is left in
the oven after cooking to dry
out and harden off.

PITTAS & KOULOURIA

PITTA BREAD

The same dough mixture is also used to make a bread ring called KOULOURIA, which is covered in sesame seeds and smaller bite-sized versions are called KOULOURAKIA; both are formed by using a sausage shape piece of dough and joining the ends together.

To make ELIOPITTA, which is olive bread, olives, onions and small pieces of potato are added to the basic bread recipe.

To make HALOUMOPITTA, which is cheese bread, small cubes of HALLOUMI are added to the basic bread recipe. Form the PITTAS by rolling the dough into a fat sausage and then curling them around.

All these versions using the basic bread recipe need to be left to rise and double in size before baking in the oven. 200C/gas mark 6 for about 35 minutes or until golden brown.

Freshly baked, these are all often sold by street vendors in the cities from a barrow as a quick and tasty snack.

This dough also can be used to make PITTA bread, once proven. It is extremely easy, as I discovered. Just take a piece of dough about the size of a peach and flatten it out with the heel of your hand on a floured board. Keep pushing the dough outwards and flattening it until it's about 0.5cm thick Heat a skillet until it is very hot and cook the PITTA for a few minutes until it turns brown, then turn it over and cook the other side. The PITTA will naturally separate in the middle.

MAKING YOUR OWN STARTER

Traditionally to make your own starter you would get Holy Water, which has been blessed by the priest on 14 September, Holy Cross Day. Alternatively you can use tap water.

Put a small amount of bread flour in a cup with some water. Beat it to get in some air and leave it in a warm place, covered, until the next day when you add a bit more flour and water. Do this every day for several days; traditionally it is said it must be an odd number five or seven. The natural airborne yeasts settling on the flour produce the fermentation and the liquid appears full of bubbles. The starter can be kept going indefinitely by adding more flour and water each time some is used.

A starter can also be made using chick peas and this is a speciality in the village of OMODHOS where they are famous for the ARKATENA KOULOURIA. The chick peas are soaked for several hours frequently whisking the water and then adding the flour to the water to achieve the starter. Ginger, cinnamon, cloves, MASTICHA and MECHLEPI together with sugar and rosewater are added to the dough to give the ARKATENA KOULOURIA its unique taste.

PASTA AND PASTRY

Aunt Eugenia showed us a how to make a wide variety of foods that all use a basic dough. These include several types of pasta:

RAVIOLES

TRIN

TOMACHIA

PHIDHE

As well as:

KOULOUROUTHKIA

BOUREKIA TIS SATCHES

BOUREKIA ANARIS

PITTES DIPLES

PITTES MONES

BASIC PASTA DOUGH

250g plain white flour
250g wholemeal flour
Pinch of salt
Pinch of ground MASTICHA
Pinch of MECHLEPI
Pinch of cinnamon (cinnamon is only used for sweet recipes)
1 tablespoon of sunflower oil
Water to mix into stiff dough (approximately 284ml)

Mix all the dry ingredients together then add the oil and mix in water to gradually bring together the ingredients to form a stiff dough. Knead the dough really well on a board for about 10 minutes or until it is smooth and elastic; the secret of good pasta dough is in the kneading. Leave to rest for at least 2 hours or keep in the fridge in a polythene bag for use the next day.

RAVIOLES

RAVIOLES use the basic pasta dough recipe (see page116) without cinnamon and with eggs to create a richer version. Traditionally served on Saturday for lunch when a chicken was boiled and the resulting stock used to cook the RAVIOLES or MACARONIA, which are then eaten with yoghurt.

Egg pasta dough

200g plain flour
2 large eggs
Pinch of salt
1 tablespoon sunflower oil
Pinch of MASTICHA
Pinch of MECHLEPI

Filling

1 HALLOUMI cheese, finely grated
Handful of fresh mint, finely chopped
2 eggs
Pinch of cinnamon

To make the pasta dough sift the flour into a bowl, crack the eggs into the centre together with the other ingredients and mix together, first with a fork and then by hand to form a stiff dough. Auntie kneaded the dough in a large bowl but I find it easier on a well-floured board. Knead the dough really well for 10 to 15 minutes or until it is smooth and elastic. Place in a cool place to rest for at least 30 minutes.

For the filling, mix all the ingredients together in a bowl to achieve a fairly stiff consistency, and if necessary add some more grated HALLOUMI.

When you are ready to make the RAVIOLEs cut the dough into quarters, and place one quarter on a floured board. Knead a little more into a ball.

Aunt Eugenia uses a long plain round rolling pin, 4cm diameter and about 46cm long, to roll her pasta and, given her many years of experience, she is an expert in rolling the pasta very thinly. The secret, she tells us, is in keeping the board and pasta well floured so that it doesn't stick. At the beginning roll out into a round and keep quarter turning the pasta to allow it to be rolled evenly. Once the pasta dough has become big enough Auntie showed us the technique of wrapping the dough around the pin and rolling backwards and forwards. This is a very good way of getting very thin pastry and is the local technique for making filo pastry. It also makes excellent use of a limited work surface as you are rolling several layers at the same time. But this takes practice and a long rolling pin. You also need a fairly good size pastry board or surface. When the pastry is about 2mm thin you can start to put your filling down.

Using a teaspoon place a row of small firm mounds of filling spaced about 2cm apart and about 4–5cm. in from the edge, but this is dependent on the size of cup or glass that you're using as a cutter. Then fold the edge of the pastry over the top of the mounds. Firm down the pasta dough in front and between the mounds, then use an espresso coffee cup or small glass to make small half-moon shapes, this also seals the two edges of the pasta parcels together.

If you are cooking your RAVIOLES immediately then set them aside on another board or plate. Don't pile them on top of each other as they might stick together.

They only take a few minutes to cook, either in boiling chicken stock to give them an extra delicious flavour, or water. Add a little olive oil if using water to prevent the RAVIOLES sticking together while cooking. When the RAVIOLES are cooked remove with a slotted spoon and sprinkle with some grated Parmesan or HALLOUMI before eating.

If you want to store them to use later, they can be frozen. For this you'll need to place them in tight rows on a thin chopping board or tray, and layered with sheets of greaseproof paper in between, before placing them in the freezer. When they are frozen the RAVIOLES can be taken out and put into bags, sealed and replaced in the freezer until wanted.

They cook in about 5 minutes from frozen but always check that they are cooked through before removing from the water.

Any leftover pastry can be made into pasta, although you need to do this immediately because the dough becomes hard if it is left. Knead all the pieces together again and roll out as before.

TRIN

This is slightly trickier and again takes practice to perfect but the finished product should look like tagliatelli, which are long thin ribbons of pasta. This is achieved by rolling the pastry very thinly by wrapping the dough around the pin and rolling backwards and forward, don't forget to use plenty of flour on your pasta and board. While the dough is still wrapped around the rolling pin, slide it carefully off the pin then cut into thin sections about 1cm wide. These are then put in a sieve. Placing the rolling pin across the middle of the sieve hold the sieve and the pin, you tip it away from you shaking the pasta toward the back of the sieve, then gently toss the pasta toward you over the rolling pin. This separates the ribbons and shakes out any excess flour.

Androula and I both had fun trying this technique but it definitely takes some practice. Then the TRIN needs to be left to dry. We put all our pasta on a clean tablecloth and TSESTOS, spreading it out as much as possible so the air could get to it and left it all to dry. Once dry it can be stored in jars. Traditionally TRIN is cooked in boiling water, then placed in milk, heated and served sprinkled with sugar or honey and eaten for breakfast. In Cyprus, this dish is usually eaten 50 days after Ascension. You can use TRIN the same way as you would any other pasta by cooking it until it is al dente and tossed in the sauce of your choice.

TOMACHIA

These are squares of pasta about 5cm square. After rolling the pasta thinly, wrap it around the pin, cut along the middle to make strips, then across to make large squares. These are shaken in the sieve, as the TRIN to remove the excess flour and then separated. These can be cooked in chicken stock and eaten with chicken, grated HALLOUMI and yoghurt.

Alternatively the TOMACHIA can be cooked, and layered one on top of each other, with a little grated ANARI sprinkled over each square as you go. A little chopped onion fried in olive oil can be sprinkled over the top of the pile.

These can also be filled, like the RAVIOLES, and sealed using a fork to press around the edges and cooked in the same manner. They can also be dried and stored or frozen.

PHIDHE

These are very small pieces of pasta rolled between the fingers until they are the size of a large grain of rice and then dried for later use.

KOULOUROUTHKIA

These are little rings of dough cooked and soaked in carob syrup. Eaten as a sweet they are a great favourite with my cousins.

Using the basic pasta dough recipe (see page 116) without the cinnamon, roll out the pasta into thin sausage-shaped lengths and make small rings by joining the ends together. Sprinkle with sesame seeds and cook in boiling water until al dente.

For a quantity made using 250g of flour, 300ml of syrup would be required as a guideline. The syrup is made using half water and half carob syrup, heat and then place the cooked rings into the mixture, turn off the heat.

Leave the rings in the syrup as long as you like.

Right Auntie
Eugenia making
KOULOUROUTHKIA

BOUREKIA TIS SATCHES

SATCHES is a Turkish word for the shallow glazed earthenware dish that is traditionally used to cook these savoury filled pasties.

Use the same basic pasta dough recipe for the cases (see page 116) without the cinnamon.

Makes approximately 12–15 pasties

Filling
Olive oil for cooking
1 onion, finely chopped
1 whole HALLOUMI, grated
Handful of mint, finely chopped
Black pepper

Fry the onion in olive oil until golden then mix with the HALLOUMI, mint and black pepper in a bowl. The quantities depend on how many you want to make of course but as a guideline use the same quantities as for the RAVIOLES (see page 117).

The same process is used for these as used to make RAVIOLES. A large cup or glass is needed to use as your cutter and give the edges an extra seal by pressing them down with the tines of a fork.

These are cooked in a dry pan, such as a cast iron skillet, which is heated until it hot and then the BOUREKIA are turned until they are cooked on all side, including the edges, until brown.

Aunt Eugenia had her own method of doing this by skewering all the BOUREKIA together and resting the skewer on the edges of the pan so that the edges alone touched the hot surface.

BOUREKIA ANARIS

These are delicious sweet little parcels of delight often eaten at parties.

Using the Basic Pasta dough quantities given should make approximately 30 parcels.

Filling
*250g soft white unsalted fresh ΛΝΛRI (a firm
ricotta could be used if this isn't available)
½ teaspoon cinnamon
1 teaspoon caster sugar
Few drops of rosewater
Few drops of vanilla essence or vanilla sugar
Zest of 1 orange*

Make a quantity of pasta using the basic pastry dough recipe (see page 116) leaving out the ΜΕCHLEPI and ΜΑSTICHΑ.

Mix all the ingredients for the filling together in a bowl. Roll out the pasta thinly and use the same process of placing the filling in rows on the pasta and cutting into half moon shapes or rounds if you prefer. These are fried in hot sunflower oil until golden.

You can also fill these with a savoury mixture of fried onion, mince and mint instead of the ΛΝΛRI.

PITTES DIPLES
(DOUBLE PIES)

This uses the basic pasta dough recipe (see page 116) and the dough is rolled out thinly. Oil, sugar and cinnamon are sprinkled over the dough and rolled over and over into a cigar shape, cut into sections, and the ends joined together and rolled flat.

Sometimes chopped nuts or tahini are put inside. The PITTIES DIPLES are fried in sunflower oil until they are golden brown.

PITTES MONES

This means PITTES on their own as they are just single rounds of pastry rolled thinly, which are fried in sunflower oil and sprinkled with sugar.

KOLOKOPITTAS
(PUMPKIN PIES)

Before I leave this section there is another pie I must mention the KOLOKOPITTA, which is very traditional. These little pies are a delight because they are savoury and yet sweet and can satisfy hunger at any time of day. I fondly remembered eating these in Cyprus so I felt I must include this recipe, which tastes just as I remember them. I have added a little MASTICHA although this isn't traditionally used in this recipe. Interestingly the filling includes fennel, which gives them a complex flavour that I love. The bulgur wheat is added to soak up the moisture from the pumpkin and sometimes rice is used instead. I prefer to use shortcrust pastry although in Cyprus, the pastry is usually made with oil not butter, producing a harder pastry. I know traditionally plain flour is used for pastry but I like self-raising as it makes it a bit lighter.

Left Rosie's clay ovens

Makes approximately 24–30 pies

For the shortcrust pastry
500g self raising flour
250g butter straight from the fridge
Pinch of salt
3–4 tablespoons of cold water

Filling
1 kilo pumpkin, peeled and chopped
1 bulb fennel, finely chopped
180g bulgur wheat
2 tablespoons raisins
2 tablespoons olive oil or sunflower oil
50g almonds, finely chopped
3 heaped tablespoons brown muscovado sugar
Good pinch or two of salt and a grinding or two of pepper
2 teaspoons cinnamon
3 grains MASTICHA crushed (optional)

Sift the flour in a bowl and cut up the butter into small pieces into the flour. With your fingertips rub the butter into the flour until it resembles fine breadcrumbs, add the salt, then add the water a spoonful at a time and mix lightly into a firm dough. The more water is added the tougher the pastry so go carefully. Leave to chill in the refrigerator for 30 minutes while you prepare the filling.

First prepare the pumpkin. I was given some Crown Prince Squash, which has a very sweet flavour and worked perfectly for these pies, but any pumpkin will do. The skins are usually very tough so using a sharp knife cut into manageable sections, then cut into slices and remove the pith and pips and cut away the tough skin with the knife. Dice the flesh into pieces no bigger than 1cm square as if the pieces are too big they won't cook through. In a large bowl add together all the ingredients and mix well so the sugar and oil are well distributed.

Preheat the oven gas mark 6/220C

Roll out the pastry thinly and cut into rounds using a small plate or dish about 15cm diameter as your guide. Fill the centre with the filling. Draw over half of the circle and seal the edges using the tines of a fork. Place on an oiled or floured cooking tray and pierce the case with a fork to let out the steam while cooking. Cook in the oven for 30 minutes until golden brown.

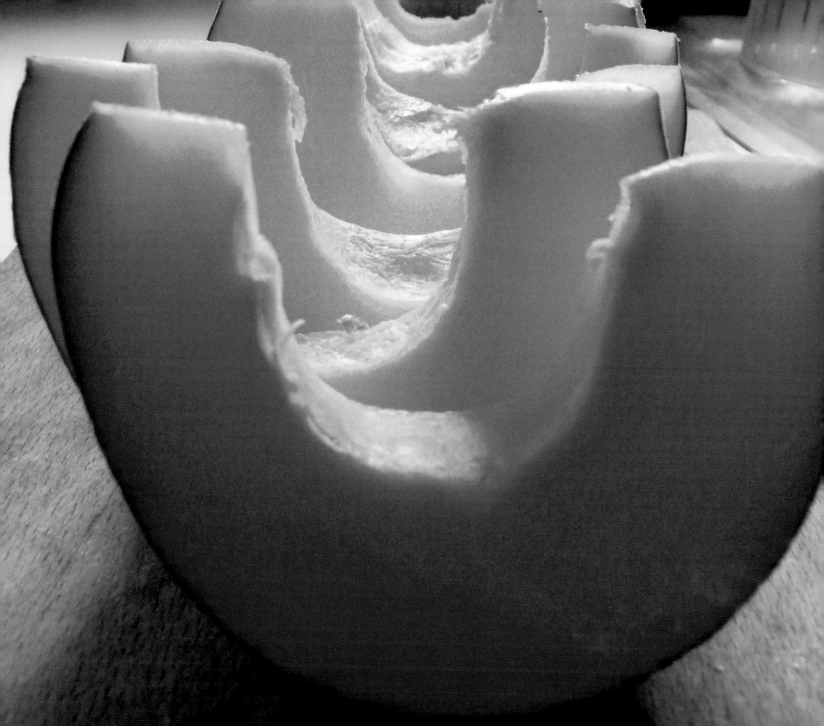

Fruit &
Vegetables

The fruit and vegetables grown on Cyprus are many and varied. As you would expect, you will find all the usual suspects growing in this moderate climate: lemons, oranges and all things citrus, as well as piles of tumbling melons in season, walnuts and almonds, pomegranates, cherries and dates as well as groves of bananas around the PAFOS region. More unusual fruits are the prickly pear, decoratively sprouting around the edges of the leaves on huge cactus like bushes, which grow everywhere on the island. If you are tempted to pick them, take care because true to their name they are covered in tiny needles, which can be extremely irritating and virtually invisible to the naked eye. Use a cloth to hold them and rub the needles off with a leaf before cutting in half to access the juicy interior.

One of my father's favourites were MESPILAS (loquats). Related to medlars they contain mostly stones but the flesh, what there is of it, is delicious. If you visit any of the food markets in Cyprus you will find all manner of produce brought down by small individual growers to sell, including these small fruits in season, which is generally around May time.

Vegetables traditionally made up the larger part of the Cypriot diet and only a small quantity of meat was consumed. There are a wide variety of greens that grow wild in the countryside: such as wild artichoke, which is the earliest cultivated vegetable on Cyprus, wild asparagus and wild spinach, STROUFOUTHKIA, which is quite bitter, it's name translated means 'little sparrows'. This is blanched and then added to scrambled eggs. My father used to cook this for us when we were children, substituting spinach for the STROUFOUTHKIA. In these modern times it is still common for Cypriots to make use of this free food, which is bursting with nutrients.

The cauliflower, KOUNOUPIDHI, is also of great historical importance, as it has been cultivated on the island for centuries and is thought by some to have been introduced to Europe from Cyprus by the Genoese sailors. There are some favourite recipes whose star ingredient is the vegetable, like

COLOCASSI, a species of taro which is a speciality of Cyprus.

Many vegetables are stuffed with a rice and meat mixture, which I have given in the KOUPEPIA recipe here. The following vegetables can all be stuffed and collectively these are called YEMISTA:

KOLOKUTHI	marrow
PIPERIA	pepper
MELITZANA	aubergine
TOMATA	tomato
KOUPEBIA	vine leaves (stuffed)
ANTHOUS KOLOKYTHION	courgette flower
KOLOKUTHAKI	courgette
KREMMUDI	onion

KOUPEPIA
(STUFFED VINE LEAVES ALSO KNOWN AS DOLMADES IN GREECE)

Vine leaves can be picked fresh when the vine is producing leaves. Pick quite young leaves as the older ones are tougher. Take the stalks off right up to the leaf and blanch them in boiling water for a few seconds until they just change colour. They can then be frozen for later use by placing a small flat pile of about five leaves onto some kitchen foil and rolling them up tightly. Seal over the ends and keep in the freezer until needed.

The following recipe was given to me by Ioanna my cousin Michael's wife and pine nuts can be substituted for the meat if you want to make a vegetarian version.

25 fresh vine leaves

Filling
½ kilo minced pork or lamb
1 onion, finely chopped
1 tablespoon parsley, finely chopped
200g long grain rice
Few sprigs of fresh mint, finely chopped
Salt and pepper
1 tablespoon olive oil
1 large fresh tomato, grated, or some tomato paste
Squeeze of lemon juice

Mix all the stuffing ingredients together except for the tomato. Blanch the vine leaves and then lay each leaf individually on a board placing a small amount of filling near the stalk end, then roll up the leaf tucking the sides in as you go. Place a small amount of olive oil in the bottom of a casserole and closely pack the vine leaf parcels together in the bottom with the end of the leaf underneath to prevent them unravelling. Drizzle with olive oil and grate the tomato over the top or some tomato paste diluted with a little water. Add enough water to just cover the KOUPEPIA and a squeeze of lemon juice. Place a plate upside down on top of the KOUPEPIA to help keep them in place, cover with a lid and cook on a low heat for 1 hour.

The same stuffing mixture can be used for all the YEMISTA recipes with the addition of the tomato to the filling. Minced lamb, beef or pork can be used or a half and half mixture of any two. The lemon juice helps cut through the fattiness of the pork and lamb. Stuffed tomatoes, peppers, aubergines, onions and courgettes can all be cooked in the same manner by slicing off the tops, or in half. Scoop out the pulpy flesh and mix with the rest of the stuffing ingredients and fry in a little oil until the liquid has been absorbed and the meat browned. The vegetables are filled with the mixture, placed in a dish with about 1cm of water in the bottom and cooked in a moderate oven gas mark 5/190C for about 1 hour until the vegetables are cooked. It is important to keep checking the water, as you don't want the dish to dry out during cooking.

XIDHATA (PICKLES)

Another major part of the traditional Cypriot diet were ΧΙΔΗΑΤΑ – (pickles) as they are an excellent way of preserving many of the abundant vegetables grown in season so that they can be enjoyed in the winter. The foods commonly pickled were: capers (flowers, stalks, leaves and fruits), carrots, cucumbers, mushrooms, peppers, cauliflower, olives, partridge eggs, rabbit and hare.

Here are a few vegetable based recipes given to me by relatives and friends.

BAMIES (LADIES FINGERS)

Serves 2 as a side dish
1 tablespoon of olive oil for frying
1 small onion, finely chopped
250g of ΒΑΜΙΕΣ
200g tinned tomatoes or 2 large tomatoes, chopped or grated
Salt and pepper

ΒΑΜΙΕΣ need to be treated carefully as they become slimy if the skin is damaged. Wash and dry well and, if necessary, only cut the end of the stalk off not the whole end. Rosie told me that if cooked from frozen they are much easier.

Fry the onion in olive oil until soft then add the ΒΑΜΙΕΣ, stir and then add either fresh or tinned tomatoes and season with salt and pepper to taste. Cook on a low heat for about 25 minutes or until the ΒΑΜΙΕΣ are tender.

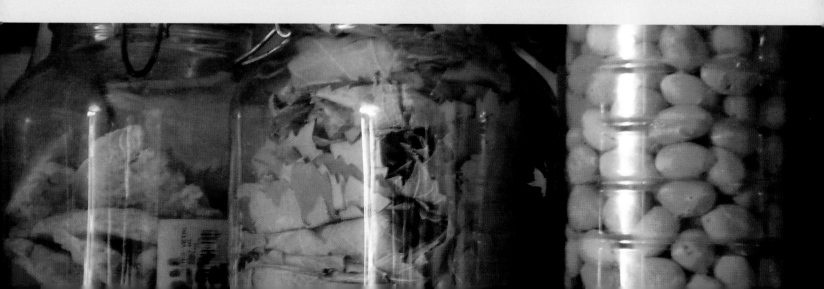

PATATES KAI POULES

This is another recipe Aunt Eugenia cooked for us and one of Androula's favourites.

Peel the POULES (baby COLOCASSI) and new potatoes. Slice the potatoes through partially to allow them to cook all the way through. The COLOCASSI can be sliced if a little large but the potatoes remain whole. Heat some light oil, such as sunflower, in a large casserole dish and fry the potatoes, allowing enough room for them to be separated, when golden add the POULES. When they are both cooked, drain the oil from the pan, add a little salt and some crushed coriander seeds with a little red wine. Cover the pan and shake, then remove the lid and leave for a few minutes to cook further. Serve immediately.

Another very simple dish eaten a lot is KOLOKUTHIA (marrows), which are boiled and eaten with oil and lemon with salt and pepper to taste.

PULSES

Another fundamental part of the diet is the pulses or OSPRIA (dried beans).

KOUKIA (BROAD BEANS)

Fresh or dried broad beans can be used for this recipe. Cook the shelled broad beans or the dried beans first and then drain.

Heat some olive oil in a deep-sided pan and add crushed or chopped garlic to your taste, and gently fry. Add some wine vinegar (about 142ml for two people) and a little flour and stir to thicken slightly, then add the broad beans. Leave for a few minutes to absorb the flavours and serve at once. More olive oil, garlic and fresh mint can be added to your taste.

LOUVI (BLACK EYE BEANS)

These are bought dried but still in their shells and are another great favourite cooked with LAHANA, a large green leaf vegetable, which is rather like Swiss chard.

The beans are shelled and cooked by first putting them in cold water and bringing them to the boil. Drain and place in clean boiling water to finish cooking; usually about 30 minutes. If you want to add LAHANA, chop the leaves coarsely and add to the beans just before they have finished cooking. When the beans are cooked, strain off the water, add lemon juice, salt, pepper and olive oil.

My dad liked the addition of raw chopped onion with this dish but sometimes a little fried onion is sprinkled on top. This is quite often eaten with cooked fish or tinned tuna.

FAGES MOUTCHENTRA
(LENTILS AND RICE)

This is another very simple but really filling and nutritious dish. A favourite of my brother.

Serves 4

The traditional ratio is 3 measures of lentils to 1 measure of rice
200g long grain rice
600g lentils (small green/brown variety)
1 onion, finely sliced
Olive oil for frying
Salt

Wash the lentils and place in a saucepan with enough water to cover them and cook for 10 minutes. Drain and place them back in the pan with the rice and enough freshly boiled water to cover, season with salt and pepper and simmer with the lid on for 15 to 20 minutes until the rice is cooked. Check during cooking that there is sufficient water to prevent burning. Meanwhile slice the onion finely and fry with a pinch of salt in the olive oil until crisp. When the rice and lentils are cooked, drain and place in a dish and pour over the oil left over from cooking the onions then sprinkle the onions on top to serve.

FASOLIA (BEANS)

In the winter pulses are eaten often, as they are both filling and nutritious. Here is a method of cooking beans, which I learned from my father and use a lot. Any type of dried bean can be used but black eye, butter beans or Puy lentils work best.

Serves 4

1 tablespoon olive oil
1 onion
1 clove garlic
2 large carrots
2 sticks of celery
400g Puy lentils
4 rashers streaky bacon (optional)
1tablespoon sun dried tomato paste
400g tinned tomatoes or passata (sieved tomato) or 3 large fresh tomatoes, grated or chopped
852ml water
Salt and pepper
Thyme and marjoram, to taste

First cook the beans. Larger ones, like butter beans will need soaking for several hours before cooking. Black eye beans need to be precooked but not soaked. If you are using Puy lentils no precooking is necessary but use the amount of water listed in the ingredients above. If you are using precooked beans and fresh tomatoes use 284ml water.

Heat some olive oil in a casserole, add some finely chopped onion and cook until soft. Cut the bacon into small pieces and add to the onion to cook for a few minutes until golden. Finely slice some carrot and celery and add to the pan then cook for a few more minutes to soften. Next add some crushed garlic, then the tomato, either fresh (chopped or grated) or tinned tomatoes or passata I like to add some sun dried tomato paste to give the dish a bit of extra depth and this should be mixed with the water before adding. If you are using fresh tomatoes allow them to soften before adding the beans. Add your cooked beans or lentils and water. If you are using cooked beans and tinned tomatoes, add just a small amount of extra water, another 140ml, then season with salt and pepper, thyme or marjoram depending on your taste. Cover with a lid and cook on a low heat for about 25 minutes covered. The Puy lentils need 40 to 45 minutes of cooking time to become tender. Check from time to time while cooking that there is enough liquid and add a little water if necessary.

This dish can be eaten straight away but I think the beans taste even better the next day.

FISH

Fish is my preferred choice whenever I eat out and particularly in Cyprus. As you would expect, being an island, Cyprus has an abundance of fish and you are spoilt for choice whether you want to catch it, buy it to cook yourself or have it cooked for you. Whenever I go to stay near Latchi near POLIS, I look forward to eating my absolute favourite meal: KALAMARI (squid) and chips with a Greek salad washed down with that unbeatable Keo beer at Yangos' tavern. It never fails to delight. Here, as in many coastal restaurants, there is a selection of fresh fish to choose from, which has been caught that day.

When buying fish at a supermarket or fish shop you are met with an exotic array: OCTAPODI (octopus), which literally translates as 'eight legs', sprawling next to squid and cuttlefish, with little whitebait huddled in a pile next to colourful red mullet and parrotfish. Then there's tuna, also known as tunny, grey mullet, bream and bass.

In Greek they are called as follows:

BARBOUNI	red mullet
FANGRI	king sea bream
KEFALOS	grey mullet
LAVRAKI	sea bass
MINERI	tunny
MARIDHA	whitebait
PESTROFA	trout
SOUPIES	cuttlefish
TSIPOURA	gilt head bream

Trout are farmed in the TROODOS MOUNTAINS and bass and bream are farmed on the coast.

I didn't acquire any fish recipes from my family or friends but when it comes to fish, my sentiment is the simpler the better. If the fish is fresh it will speak for itself; I don't mean that literally of course, as that would be a little unnerving! The larger fish often need just to be cleaned, rubbed with lemon, salt and pepper, drizzled with oil and either grilled or stuffed with dill or fennel, wrapped in foil and cooked in the oven or over charcoal. Smaller fish, such as whitebait, are great fried. Octopus is often cooked in a KRASATO dish with red wine as is CALAMARI, but the latter is more commonly cut into rings and fried in a light batter. Cuttlefish can be stuffed or cooked in red wine also.

Meat

The following recipes give an illustration of a few of the most popular meat dishes cooked in Cyprus. Many of them can be cooked on top of the stove a reflection of the traditional method used of cooking on a trivet over the fire. Dishes such as KLEFTICO are great cooked in the clay ovens outside. This is one of those very popular Greek dishes found everywhere in tavernas and restaurants. It literally translates as 'stolen' and the story of its origins is as well known as the dish itself.

Left KLEFTICO

KLEFTICO

In 1821 during the Greek uprising against the Ottoman Empire, the rebels hid in the hills. They stole meat from the villagers, both Greek and Turk, as they had no other access to food. To avoid detection while it was cooking, they dug a hole in the ground to light a fire. When the wood had turned to charcoal, they laid the meat on some large leaves on top of the charcoal together with some wild herbs and covered the whole thing over with more leaves and earth. The meat cooked there as long as necessary while the rebels went about their... well... rebelling. When they returned after a hard day's toil they would find the meat tender and falling off the bone. Cooked this way it never burned and stayed warm for hours.

Nowadays, to get the same result, the meat is cooked in a clay pot or TAVAS (see page 143) in a clay oven, The process of cooking KLEFTICO is much the same one as used by the rebels: the meat, preferably mutton or shoulder of lamb, including the bones and fat as this adds flavour and supplies the juices, is cut into large pieces. The lamb and some peeled potatoes (the weight of the potatoes should be equal to the meat) are placed in the pot, together with plenty of bay leaves, rosemary or oregano, salt and pepper, a quartered lemon and a drizzle of olive oil. Mix everything together well with your hands. You

can, if you choose, pour a little water into the bottom of the pot to give extra moisture while everything is cooking. The pot is sealed tightly with either a close-fitting lid or aluminum foil tightly fixed over the top.

The pot can either be cooked in a clay oven or in a pre-heated oven, gas mark 8/225C, then just before putting the pot in the oven, turn down the temperature to gas mark 4/180C and leave to cook for 1½ to 2 hours, then reduce the heat to gas mark 2/150C for a further hour. Finally turn down the oven to its lowest gas mark ¼/100C until you are ready to eat. The meat is deliciously tender and you'll find a quantity of rendered fat and juices at the bottom of the pot, which should be saved for later use, such as making PILAFI (see page 110).

If you haven't got a special unglazed casserole, you can obtain a similar result either by wrapping the meat, herbs and potatoes tightly in kitchen foil, first lined with greaseproof paper, or using an ordinary casserole and sealing the lid tight with either foil under the lid or a pastry seal around the edge.

This recipe is a typical example of Greek cooking in general, as the quantities and ingredients are adjusted according to what is available, your preferences and how many people you want to feed. As a guide use 1 kilo of meat to feed 4 people.

YIACHNI

This name is given to any stew, both meat and vegetable, using a tomato sauce.

This recipe was given to me by Androula and chicken can be substituted for pork if you prefer. Cauliflower, KOUNOUPIDHI can be added or substituted for the meat to make a vegetarian option.

Serves 2

Lamb pieces, chops, 2 cutlets per person or
1 chump chop per person
2 tablespoons olive oil
2 onions, halved
1 garlic clove, crushed
2 large potatoes, peeled and cut into quarters
250g peas or young beans, depending on your taste
2 medium carrots, sliced
1 stick celery, sliced
400g tinned tomatoes or 2 large fresh tomatoes
quartered
1 bay leaf
Salt and pepper

Heat the olive oil and brown the meat on all sides to seal the juices. Add the garlic, onions, carrots, celery, potatoes and peas and give them a good stir to cover them in the juices and cook gently for a few minutes to soften, stirring occasionally. If you are using fresh tomatoes add at this stage to allow them to soften. Add the bay leaf, salt and pepper to taste, together with the tinned tomatoes and some water to just cover the contents. Give it all a good stir again and cover with a lid. Leave on a low heat for 1½ to 2 hours until the juices are thickened and the meat falls away from the bone. Neck of lamb would work very well in this recipe. To add a little more depth of flavour some cinnamon and CHINIA (berries of the schinos tree) can be added together with a teaspoon of sugar, which reduces the acidity of the tomatoes.

COLOCASSI TIS CHRISTINAS

COLOCASSI is a species of the taro family, it has large leaves and a tuberous conical-shaped root and is eaten in various forms widely in Asia, the Caribbean, as well as Africa and Egypt. The Cypriot variety is available from September to June.

This recipe was given to me by Christina, as it is a speciality of hers and this recipe works with both chicken and pork. Christina cooks this dish in a pressure cooker which she highly recommends.

Serves 4
4 large chicken pieces or 750g pork.
2 or 3 COLOCASSI
2 or 3 lemons
Leaves of 4 celery stalks and some stalk, finely chopped
2 medium onions, finely chopped
1 x 400g tin tomatoes or tomato juice or
3 large fresh tomatoes
Salt
Pepper
1 stick of cinnamon
1–2 tablespoons olive oil for cooking the meat

COLOCASSI is another vegetable that needs careful handling and should be washed and then dried thoroughly. Peel it, but once it is peeled avoid wetting it again as it becomes slimy, only wipe with dry kitchen paper towel. Chip rather than cut into small pieces, to avoid it becoming slimy, and add plenty of lemon juice; 1 lemon per 1 large COLOCASSI. Put a little olive oil on the meat and grill until brown. Then place in the pressure cooker together with the celery, onions and tomatoes. Add the juice of two lemons, together with some water so it just covers the contents and cook for approximately 25 minutes.

Alternatively, fry the meat in a pan with the oil and when brown add the celery and onions to brown, then all the other ingredients then cover and cook on a low heat until tender, approximately 1 hour.

TAVAS

This dish takes its name from the pot in which it is cooked. The pot is a particular unglazed clay variety that has to be prepared by cooking pork fat in it for several hours. This process seals the pot and lends an extra depth of flavour to whatever is then subsequently cooked. This is the same dish as is used when cooking KLEFTICO (see page140) It should not be washed in soap and water once used but just wiped clean. TAVAS can be cooked with either lamb or rabbit and the cumin gives the dish a very distinctive taste. Rosie gave me the following recipe.

Serves 4

1 rabbit cut into portions or 500g of lamb, preferably on the bone such as chops
3 large onions, finely chopped
½ kilo small tomatoes, halved
3 large potatoes, sliced
Salt and pepper
1 tablespoon sunflower or olive oil
1 teaspoon cumin seeds

Put all the ingredients into your TAVAS if you have one or otherwise a casserole dish. Put in enough water to cover the bottom of the dish. This dish is cooked covered in the oven for 1½ to 2 hours on low gas mark 4/180C. Stir occasionally during cooking and then take the lid off toward the end of the cooking time to allow the contents to brown. The meat should fall off the bone and the sauce thickened.

A regional version, Levkaritikos TAVAS uses rice instead of potatoes.

STIFADO

Rosie gave me this recipe and she recommends using hare but I use rabbit and it has become a firm favourite. The vinegar and cinnamon add subtle flavours to the rabbit and the large quantity of shallots used add sweetness. This recipe is quite delicious and very simple to make. In restaurants you will often find this dish made with beef.

Serves 4

1 rabbit or hare
500g shallots, whole, or onions, quartered (usually the weight of onions equals the weight of meat)
500g potatoes, (optional) peeled and quartered, or left whole if small
1 teaspoon whole black peppercorns
2 bay leaves
1 stick cinnamon
300ml red wine
140ml red wine vinegar
1 dessertspoon tomato puree, thinned with water, or 284ml passata (sieved tomato)
Salt
2 tablespoons olive oil for cooking

Cut the rabbit or hare into pieces and fry in a little oil until golden then take out and put aside. Peel the shallots or onions, if using onions cut them into quarters but leave the shallots whole, cut the potato add to the juices in the pan and cook until the onions are soft. Put the meat back into the pan and add the peppercorns, salt, bay leaves, cinnamon, red wine and wine vinegar together with the tomato juice or puree. The liquid should cover the meat so add a little water if required. Taste and adjust the seasoning, then cover and leave to cook on a low heat or cook in a moderate oven gas mark 5/190C for 1½ to 2 hours until the meat falls from the bone and the juices are reduced.

KRASATO

Wine is not only used as a way of preserving meat but also in cooking. KRASATO is the name given to dishes cooked with wine to add flavour to the sauce. Below are a couple of recipes that were given to me but are by no means the whole range of Cypriot recipes using wine. Chicken is quite often cooked in a casserole with wine and potatoes, as is beef and both are delicious. One of my favourite dishes using wine is octopus.

AFELIA

This is a very simple and tasty dish that Androula cooked for me.

Either use cubed pork meat or chops, it must have a little fat as this gives the final dish flavour as, of course, does the bone in the chops.

Serves 2
2 large pork chops
1 teaspoon coriander seeds
1 teaspoon cumin seeds
300ml red wine
2 tablespoon olive oil
1 dessertspoon tomato puree

Cover the meat in red wine, crushed coriander and cumin and leave to marinate and absorb the flavours for 2 hours or 2 days in the fridge; the longer you leave it the richer the flavour.

When you are ready to cook the dish, heat some olive oil in a frying pan and sauté the meat until it is brown and cooked through. Add the marinade juices to the pan and cook until it starts to bubble then turn the heat down, cover and leave to cook until the juices have reduced to a thick sauce, about 40 minutes as a guide. Then add a little tomato puree.

This can be eaten with PILAFI (see page 110) or PATATES KAI POULES (see page 132).

SHEFTALIES

These are not generally cooked at home but are commonly on the menu when eating out and are one of my favourites. The combination of Cypriot meat and herbs in this sausage, cooked over charcoal is a winner in my book. On a recent trip, Angela and I went in search of lunch after our basket makers search and stopped at Klokkos restaurant in XYLOFAGOU. Spotting SHEFTALIES on the menu made it an easy choice for me. Presented with a fresh salad, some home-made TZATZIKI and PITTAS washed down with a Keo beer, this was an excellent meal and Angela hasn't stopped talking about it since!

Here is a recipe for the sausage but to get the authentic flavour they are best cooked over charcoal and you need to use a good quality meat, preferably organic.

¼ kilo of minced pork
¼ kilo of minced beef
1 tablespoon mint, chopped
1 tablespoon parsley, chopped
1 large onion, finely chopped
1 generous tablespoon breadcrumbs
Salt and pepper
Pinch of cinnamon
Pig's intestine for the casing

Mix all the ingredients together in a bowl using your hands then stuff into the pig's intestine a little at a time, keeping the meat tightly together. When you have a largish sausage (or your preferred size) twist the intestine around to seal and then cut. Twist the other end around to close. Continue making sausages until all the meat is used. Cook gently over charcoal, making sure the sausages are not too close to the charcoal or they will burn without cooking through.

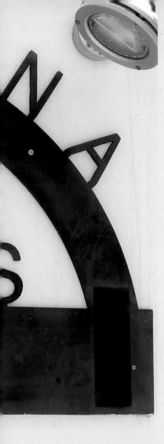

KEFTEDHES

These little nuggets are generally eaten as a finger food at parties or picnics and are served as part of a meze. Irinoula gave me this recipe.

½ kilo minced pork
3 or 4 potatoes
1 large onion
1 egg
1 tablespoon parsley (according to taste), chopped
1 tablespoon mint, finely chopped
Salt and pepper
Pinch of cinnamon
145g breadcrumbs
Sunflower oil for frying

Peel then grate the potatoes and squeeze out the water into a separate bowl keeping this aside for later. Then peel and grate the onion, salt it and add it to the potato, breadcrumbs, pork, egg, parsley, mint and pepper. Mix well together with your hands. Carefully tip away the water from the bowl with the potato liquid to leave the starch at the bottom, and add this to the meat mixture. Take a small amount of the mixture in your hands, about the size of a walnut, and shape into a flattened meat ball and shallow fry in hot sunflower oil until golden brown and cooked through. Drain on kitchen towel and pile on a plate to be eaten. They will soon disappear, as they are very moreish.

PSITO

As mentioned previously the traditional Saturday meal in Cyprus was boiled chicken with RAVIOLES or MACARONIA and yoghurt and on the Sunday it would be PSITO. This is the Cypriot version of the British Sunday roast. It is very simple but quite delicious. Any meat can be used but it's usually in large pieces not a whole joint or chicken. The meat is washed, rubbed with lemon, put in a roasting pan together with peeled and halved potatoes. Slit the potatoes down the middle to allow them to cook all the way through. Oil is added together with salt and pepper and any herbs you like and depending on the meat. Water is added to generously cover the bottom of the pan and that's it. Traditionally the roast was taken to the village baker to cook in the clay oven while you went to church but nowadays it is more common to roast it in your own oven at gas mark 6/200C for about 1½ hours. Baste it a few times to cover everything in the cooking juices. The addition of the water keeps everything moist and tender.

PASTICHIO (ALSO KNOWN AS MACARONIA TOU FOURNOU)

When we were invited to a relative's house for lunch we would always be served PSITO, PILAFI and PASTICHIO. PASTICHIO has a very similar construction to lasagne with layers of pasta and meat sauce and a béchamel-style sauce poured over it all before it is baked in the oven. This is another dish that reflects the Italian influences of the past, as PASTICCIO is the name for baked lasagne in Northern Italy. Once cooked it is cut into wedges and served cold.

Here is a basic recipe, which is my adaptation from several sources although there are variations according to taste.

250g tubular pasta, such as macaroni
1 tablespoon melted butter
40g HALLOUMI, ANARI OR PECORINO, grated
1 tablespoon breadcrumbs

Meat sauce

500g minced beef or pork, or half and half
2 tablespoons olive oil
1 medium onion, chopped finely
100ml red wine
200g tinned chopped tomatoes
1 tablespoon tomato paste or sun dried tomato sauce
1 cinnamon stick
Salt and pepper
1 tablespoon fresh mint and parsley, chopped

Crema (white sauce)

60g butter
60g plain flour
568ml milk
A pinch of nutmeg
2 egg yolks

Heat the olive oil in a frying pan and fry the onion until soft and golden, add the mince, breaking up the lumps, and cook on a high heat for a few minutes until the meat browns. Then add the wine, tomatoes and paste with mint, parsley, cinnamon stick, salt and pepper, and stir well. Add a tablespoon of water and cook over a low heat for about 35 to 40 minutes until the meat is tender and the sauce reduced. Taste and adjust seasoning if necessary.

Cook the pasta in boiling water until al dente, drain and put aside to cool.

To make the white sauce: melt the butter in a pan and then mix in the flour to make a roux. Gradually add the milk a bit at a time stirring all the while to avoid lumps. Bring to the boil stirring all the time then lower the heat and cook for 6 minutes stirring from time to time. Add the nutmeg and salt and pepper. Let it cool, then add a quarter of the sauce to the pasta and beat in the egg yolks and half the cheese, keeping the remaining sauce warm.

Preheat the oven gas to mark 4/180C.

When the meat sauce is cooked remove the cinnamon stick. Grease a shallow tin with some melted butter. Pour one third of the pasta mix into the tin and spread it out evenly, then pour half the meat sauce evenly over the pasta and repeat ending with a layer of pasta. Pour over the remaining white sauce and sprinkle with the remaining cheese and breadcrumbs. Put in the oven and cook for about 40 minutes until the top is golden and bubbly.

Leave to cool before cutting into squares and serving.

STREET FOOD & EATING IN THE COUNTRYSIDE

One of my best memories of early holidays in Cyprus was when a whole group of family members from YEROLAKKOS took us on a trip up the mountains in an old Bedford bus driven by the village bus driver. These bull-nosed buses circa 1950s were then a familiar sight all over the island providing a valuable network between the cities and villages before cars became king. Now, although a much rarer sight, they still can be seen dotted about but are kept more for sentimental value than as everyday transport. We stopped to cook SOUVLA at a designated picnic area, of which Troodos has many. Picnic tables and chairs are set out under the pine trees with a large purpose built barbecue area provided, to enable you to cook in safety and a tap nearby, supplying fresh mountain water for drinking and washing. This is picnicking in style. Large pieces of meat from goat or lamb are slowly cooked over charcoal. Salad is prepared and bread broken, a little yoghurt on the side and a more delicious meal could not exist. SOUVLA is usually cooked at weddings and other major and minor celebrations.

The mini version, which is a common street food, is SOUVLAKIA. This is the Cypriot kebab, small pieces of meat skewered and cooked over charcoal. When ready, the meat together with salad are put in a warm pitta bread making a healthy and tasty lunch. SHEFTALIES (see page 148) are sometimes mixed in with this, too.

I have already mentioned the breads, HALLOUMOPITTES and ELIOPITTES along with TAHINOPITTES the sweet version made with cinnamon and tahini, are all sold from barrows in the street. Another delicious snack available to eat on the hoof are KOUPES. These can be made at home but are quite fiddly. They have a rather fat cigar shape and are made with a bulgur wheat casing covered in breadcrumbs, filled with a meat, mint and onion mixture, which are deep-fried. Yum!

Sweet things in life

In Britain we have a long history and a rich vein of puddings and cake recipes when we're in need of that sweet treat at the end of a meal or in the middle of the morning with our coffee or in the afternoon with our tea. My mother had her own repertoire of favourite cakes and puddings, which she added to throughout her life, as she loved to experiment with new recipes. I delighted in them as a child and as an adult, I have now only fond memories of them although my sister still makes a chocolate cake the way my mother did. My father would take great pleasure in eating them as he, like me, had a sweet tooth.

Left *My cousins polishing off the* PALOUZES *in the pan*

This is why it used to be a bit of a disappointment when eating out in Cyprus to discover that the 'desserts' section was sadly lacking in variety, maybe some fruits in season and of course, for the very sweet toothed, Greek pastries, particularly the delicious GALATOPOUREKO. Most of the pastries use FILO pastry with a filling of crushed nuts and spices but GALATOPOUREKO is filled with a stiff custard made with vanilla-flavoured milk and semolina. KATAIFI looks like shredded wheat but is in fact made with special FILO dough that is shredded into strips. This gives a false impression as the Cypriots make a wide variety of sweet things and they do them in their own unique way. They might not show up on a menu but you will come across them in other situations.

The one sweet that most visitors to Cyprus will know is Turkish Delight; in Cyprus it is known as LOUKOUMIA. This word is a Greek version of the Turkish word lokum or lokma, which in turn comes from the Arabic which means 'morsel' and this little delicacy is known all over the Middle East. In Cyprus there are two main areas where LOUKOUMIA is produced, one in VEROSKIPOU near PAFOS and the other in FOINI in Troodos. It is made mostly with starch, sugar and a variety of flavourings, the most famous being rosewater, usually with the addition of nuts and is generously dusted with icing sugar. It is sometimes offered to the guests at weddings.

KOPIASTE

This is invariably the greeting you'll be met with by Cypriots when being invited to sit, talk, have coffee, or as a guest invited to a Cypriot's house. It is a greeting that means 'come and share whatever is on offer'. It is the plural of the verb KOPIAZO, which literally means 'take the trouble'. Traditionally guests would be welcomed by burning olive leaves in the KAPNISTIRI, which is used in certain ceremonies at weddings. Made of silver it has two round containers shaped like apples with the top half hinged to open up, one for charcoal and one for olive leaves. With it is the MERECHA, a container in the shape of a pear for rosewater or bitter orange water. The burning olive leaves are passed over the guest's head three times and the water is sprinkled on the palms. The olive leaves have been taken to the church on Palm Sunday and collected again on Ascension Day.

As a visitor to a Cypriot's house you will always be offered refreshment and food will usually accompany your drink (see page 93). KERASTICO is the word used to cover everything that is offered to the guest.

You will inevitably be given a GLYKO to eat at some stage, with a glass of water to wash it down. Translated it means literally, sweet and it is a good description. When in season all manner of fruits and some vegetables are preserved in a thick syrup and stored awaiting the arrival of guests. This is a very similar to the process of making jams and marmalades, but the fruit is kept whole to eat as a sweet. Cherries, bitter orange, baby aubergines with almonds in the centre are just some but my favourite is walnut. This is one of the most time-consuming GLYKOS to produce, as it takes eight days from start to finish.

When I made my first trip to Cyprus we had many relatives to visit. With every visit we were offered a GLYKO. There was absolutely no possibility of refusing this delight for fear of causing offence and by the end of the day my stomach groaned at the thought of yet another GLYKO being produced.

Irinoula talked us through the process of making the walnut and cherry GLUKOS.

Left The guests welcome; Androula's KAPNISTIRI and MERECHA with some GLYKO

WALNUT GLYKO

The walnuts are picked when green, cleaned by peeling or scraping away any hard parts. The older they are the harder they are. Gloves must be worn as walnuts stain your hands black which is why they make such an excellent natural dye. A hole is pierced through the middle using a knitting needle and then they are soaked in water for eight days, changing the water every day.

The walnuts are washed well and then boiled in a pan for 2–3 minutes. Drained and put in cold water to cool then the end is cut off and a blanched or toasted almond is inserted. The walnuts are boiled again for 3 minutes and again drained and cooled in cold water. They are boiled for a third time and after this they are tested to see if they are soft enough by pricking with a sewing needle, if it passes through they are ready for the final stages. Again the water is drained and they are put in cold water, with some lemon juice added and left to soak in this for 3–4 hours. After this the water is drained for the final time then the walnuts are put in a pan with sugar and water to make the syrup. For every 25 walnuts 1 kilo of sugar is used and 2–3 glasses (568ml–852ml) of water. They are boiled together with a cinnamon stick until the syrup thickens and then some more lemon juice is added. Finally they are put into clean jars. All these sweets are presented on a small glass dish and eaten with a small fork (BIROUNAKI) or spoon (KOUTALAKI), which are designed specifically for this purpose. I saw a beautiful example of these in a silver shop in LEFKOSIA, Nikos Ioannou, made in filigree silver, which is another traditional speciality of Cyprus.

CHERRY GLYKO

Here is Irinoula's recipe for cherry GLYKO. This recipe retains the cup measurement as given to me by Irinoula. Just be sure to use the same cup to measure both sugar and cherries as it is the ratio that is important not the cup size.

Put some water and lemon juice in bowl and add the cherries, after removing the stalks. Prepare another bowl with water and lemon juice and, after removing the pips from the cherries with a special pip-removing gadget, put them in the clean water. Take 5 cups of cherries and put in a casserole (the cherries must have room to sit side by side in the casserole). For every 5 cups of cherries add 4 cups of sugar. Pour in a very little water or rosewater to just cover the bottom of the pan. Put on a low heat and watch all the time, skimming any froth from the top. To tell if the cherries are ready, take a wooden spoon and if the syrup drips slowly off the spoon they are done.

Squeeze lemon juice over them and leave to cool before putting in sterilized jars. As you can see they are a lot simpler than the walnuts.

Left A beautiful example of silver filigree BIROUNAKIA & KOUTALAKIA *in Mr Nikos Ioannou's shop Lefkosia*

HONEY

Honey has been an important food in Cyprus for centuries. The multitude of wild herbs and flowers particularly in the Troodos Mountains, give the honey a unique quality and aroma. As you drive around you often see rows of hives lining the roads. They look to me like little chests of drawers especially as they're painted in a jolly yellow or blue and white. The traditional hive used in Cyprus was called a TZIVERTI which was a cylindrical hive made from clay or mud and straw. Beekeepers would line them along an outside wall of their house stacked on top of each other to cover a whole wall. The bee would enter the hive from outside and the householder could access the honey from the inside of his house through the wall. These types of hives are still used today in some places. Two major types of honey are produced, the first from the flowers of the aromatic herbs in summer and in the autumn the flowers of the citrus trees provide another type. There are also the very limited quantities of monofloral honey produced from wild lavender and wild thyme.

Many of the sweet pastries and cakes made in Cyprus use syrup. The following recipes give the ingredients as sugar and water but traditionally honey would have been used instead. Try it as a substitute for the sugar you will need less of it and taste the difference.

DAKTYLA TIS NITSAS

My cousin Elenitsa gave me this recipe, as she is
the one known for her sweet making in the family.
DAKTYLA translated is finger, which describes the
shape and size of these sweets.

They are usually served as part of a buffet at
christenings and other special occasions. The
quantities given will provide a big enough pile for just
such an occasion, approximately 80 to 90. They can
be eaten during Lent as they don't have either butter
or eggs in them only flour, oil and water oh… and of
course sugar!

Pastry
1 kilo plain flour
284ml of sunflower oil
1 teaspoon salt
568ml tepid water

Filling
300g almonds, finely chopped
3 tablespoon of caster sugar
2 teaspoon ground cinnamon
1 teaspoon ground cloves
1 tablespoon rosewater or orange water

Syrup

705g of caster sugar
710ml of water
1 tablespoon honey (optional)
Juice of half a lemon
500ml sunflower oil for frying

To make the syrup boil the sugar and water together with the lemon juice for 10 minutes until the sugar has dissolved and the syrup has thickened, turn off the heat then add the honey. Allow to cool.

Next make the pastry by sifting the flour and adding the sunflower oil, salt and water. Bring all the ingredients together with your hands and knead the dough well until it is smooth. Leave to rest for 1 hour.

Meanwhile chop the almonds finely and mix together with the sugar, rosewater or orange water, cinnamon and cloves.

When the pastry has rested, cut a quarter of it and roll out fairly thinly using the long thin rolling pin method used by Aunt Eugenia in the pastries section previously (see page 117). Cut into 8cm squares, about the length of your finger. Place some of the filling at one end and roll the pastry over twice so now it is also the width of your finger, then seal the ends by pressing with the tines of a fork. Continue making and place on a tray before leaving to harden and dry for about 1 to 2 hours. Fry them in very hot sunflower oil until golden and put into the syrup. Take them out of the syrup and drain, then put on to a clean plate and sprinkle with some more chopped almonds if you prefer. If you run out of filling the pastry squares can be fried and sprinkled with sugar afterward.

These keep for several days and can be frozen.

BAKLAVA

This is one of the well-known pastries throughout the Eastern Mediterannean generally bought in a ZACHAROPLASTEIO (pastry shop) in Cyprus but it is possible to make them at home. The professional pastry chefs make filo pastry from scratch and achieve a paper-thin result but this takes a lot of skill and experience and you can use ready-made FILO pastry.

Makes 12–16
500g filo pastry
350g unsalted butter, melted, or light oil
750g walnuts, crushed, and almonds, chopped small, or use any nuts to your taste – hazelnuts, pistachios, etc.

Syrup
500g caster sugar
300ml water
Dash of rosewater or orange water
Cloves or cinnamon
1 tablespoon lemon juice

First make your syrup by putting the water, cloves and sugar in a pan, heat and stir until the sugar dissolves and it starts to bubble. Cook for 7 minutes then take off the heat and add the lemon juice and rosewater, stirring it thoroughly, then allow it to cool and remove the cloves.

Pre-heat the oven to gas mark 4/180C. Grease a baking sheet and layer three or four sheets of FILO pastry on top of each other, brushing melted butter between each sheet. Sprinkle with nuts, add another sheet of FILO and sprinkle more nuts, brushing each sheet with melted butter as you go, layering until all the nuts are gone and finishing with three or four more sheets of filo pastry brushed with the butter. Fold up around the edges. Using a sharp knife cut the pastry into parallel lines and then diagonal to make diamond shaped blocks about 1½ inches wide, making sure you have cut right down to the tray. Put in the oven and cook for 25 minutes then reduce the heat to gas mark 2/150C and bake for a further 20 minutes longer until they are crisp and golden. Take out of the oven and pour over the syrup straight away and cut again along the lines previously made and leave to cool.

After all that sticky syrupy stuff here are a few cake recipes – still with syrup poured over them –but not nearly so sweet and sticky. The syrup gives the cake moistness rather than a gooey syrupy texture. All the cake recipes I have been given have a syrup mixture poured over them but the cake mixture itself has a lot less sugar to counteract this. I suspect the original reason for putting the syrup over the finished cake was to keep it moist in a climate where otherwise it would dry out very quickly. Just my theory…

REVANI TIS ANDROULAS

Androula gave me her recipe for this cake, which she told me is found all over the Middle East in different versions.

260g unsalted butter or 284ml sunflower oil
120g caster sugar
4 eggs
230g semolina
270g plain flour
110g desiccated coconut
Few drops of vanilla essence
284ml orange juice or milk
1 liqueur glass brandy

Syrup
250g sugar
426ml water
2 or 3 cloves
1 cinnamon stick
Peel of half a lemon

Pre-heat the oven to gas mark 4/180C. First make the syrup, as it has to be cold when you pour it on the cake. Combine the sugar, water, cloves and cinnamon and lemon peel in a pan, bring to the boil and cook for 10 minutes or until the syrup thickens. Remove from the heat and set aside to cool.

To make the cake, beat the butter and the sugar together in a bowl until light and creamy.

Crack the eggs separately into a bowl, whisk well until light and frothy and add this to the butter mixture little by little, then add the brandy. Mix in the coconut then, adding a little juice at a time, mix in the semolina. Finally fold in the flour and baking powder. Add the vanilla essence and a little milk if necessary to make a stiff batter-like mixture and mix well.

Grease a square (22cm) baking tin then shake some flour into it to coat evenly. Pour in the mixture and bake in the oven for 45 minutes until the cake is cooked in the middle. Take it out of the oven and pierce small holes evenly into the cake with a skewer, knitting needle or toothpick. Remove the cinnamon, cloves and peel from the syrup pour it over the cake and leave it to soak in. Sprinkle the cake with a little coconut. Serve cut into squares.

REVANI TIS SONIAS

I experimented with the REVANI and came up with my own version below. I've substituted rice flour for semolina to give it a lighter texture and it has a mild almondy flavour. The orange juice based syrup is a nice change.

125g unsalted butter
60g caster sugar
2 eggs
75g rice flour
100g plain flour
50g ground almonds
Juice of 1 large orange or 2 small ones
1 teaspoon baking powder
Few drops of almond essence
Handful of blanched almonds for the top

Syrup

Juice of 1 large orange or two small oranges
100g caster sugar

Pre-heat the oven to gas mark 4/180C.

To make the cake: sift the flour, ground rice and baking powder into a bowl. Mix the softened butter with the sugar and beat until creamy in a separate bowl. Add the almond essence. Using another bowl, whisk the eggs together. Gradually add the beaten eggs to the butter and sugar mixture and gradually also add the flour mixture. Mix together with the orange juice and add the ground almonds, and then mix well. The consistency should be a stiffish batter, if necessary add a few drops of milk. Grease a non-stick loaf tin (20cm x 10cm) and pour in the mixture. Place the blanched almonds on the top. Cook in the oven for 45 to 50 minutes or until the cake is cooked in the middle.

While the cake is baking, place the orange juice and sugar in a pan and heat until the sugar has dissolved and thickened. When the cake is cooked remove it from the oven and pierce with a knitting needle or skewer evenly all over and then pour over the syrup, and allow to soak in and cool.

SHAMALI

This is what Elenitsa says is also called a KALON PRAMA or 'a good thing'. This unusually is made with yoghurt and the semolina gives it a rather coarse texture. But it does tastes very good indeed. For a slightly lighter cake half plain flour and half semolina can be used.

4 eggs
180g caster sugar
580g semolina
200g plain yoghurt
195g butter or 213ml sunflower oil
3 or 4 granules MASTICHA, crushed
Few drops of vanilla essence
2 teaspoons baking powder
Handful of blanched almonds

Syrup
480g caster sugar
568ml water
Squeeze of lemon juice
1 cinnamon stick

Pre-heat the oven to gas mark 4/180C.

To make the cake: cream the butter and the sugar together until very creamy. Separate the egg yokes and add individually, beating well each time. Then add the yoghurt and gradually add the semolina mixing thoroughly. Mix together with the baking powder, MASTICHA and vanilla essence and beat well until all the ingredients are incorporated. Whisk the egg whites until stiff and gently fold into the mixture. The mixture should have a batter-like consistency. Pour into a shallow greased square baking tin (22cm) and put in the oven. After 10 minutes remove the cake and place the almonds on top then replace in the oven for a further 35 to 40 minutes. When the cake has turned golden, test the centre with a fork to check that it is cooked thoroughly.

While the cake is cooking make the syrup. In a pan, melt the sugar in the water and then add the cinnamon stick and lemon juice. Bring to the boil and then lower the heat and cook for 10 minutes, stirring occasionally until the syrup thickens. Remove the cinnamon stick. When the cake is cooked leave it for 10 minutes to rest then pierce evenly all over with toothpick and pour over the syrup

SWEETS ON THE STREETS

LOKMADHES

These are found on sale at holiday times from stalls that cook them on the spot. They are a firm favourite with my niece who nagged us continuously until we bought her some. Traditionally, they are cooked at home in the evening of the 5th of January to celebrate the baptism of Christ. When they are ready, there is a ritual, which involves throwing them up to the roof and reciting a little verse. Elenitsa gave me this recipe.

Dough

379ml tepid water

11g or 1 sachet dried yeast

3 tablespoons caster sugar

½ potato, cooked and mashed

½ potato, raw and grated

Pinch of salt

2 or 3 granules MASTICHA, crushed

Sunflower oil for deep-frying

Syrup

480g caster sugar

568ml water

Squeeze of lemon juice

Start by making the syrup. In a pan, melt the sugar in the water and then add the lemon juice. Bring to the boil and then lower the heat and cook for 10 minutes, stirring occasionally until the syrup thickens. Leave to cool.

To make the dough: mix all the ingredients together and leave the batter to rise and bubble for about 1 hour.

Put the oil on to heat. When it is very hot take a piece of dough and, using a teaspoon, scoop small nugget-sized pieces out. Place the nuggets in the hot oil and toss about with a ladle and keep turning them until they are a golden colour.

Remove them from the pan and drain to take off the excess oil, then put them in syrup.

Two other sweets sold at festival times are: SHAMISHI, which is made using the same dough as the LOKMADHES above but made into triangles filled with semolina custard and deep fried, and MACHALEPI, which is a refreshing blancmange like confection made with rosewater and cornstarch.

CAROB

Carob syrup is a wholly delicious product. I like to pour a little on my porridge in the morning instead of honey. It has been used as a natural sweetener in foods for centuries because of its high sugar content and the carob grown in Cyprus has a higher sugar content than any other. It contains a valuable source of nutrients, vitamins and minerals and has more calcium than milk. As well as being used to produce syrup it is also made into PASTELLI, a popular Cypriot sweet.

Carob trees are native to the Mediterranean and have been cultivated in the region for over 4,000 years. There were once 2.4 million fruit-bearing trees on the island, once known as 'the black gold of Cyprus' it was a major export and contributed greatly to the agricultural economy. The number of trees is now vastly depleted, which is due partly to the fact that the main orchards were in the north part of the island, which is now occupied by Turkey and partly that it is a labour-intensive crop to harvest.

Most carob production today is in the LARNAKA and LEMESOS districts, which is where ANOGYRA lies. Androula took me there to see a small factory, which is the only truly traditional carob factory left in Cyprus. There is also a small museum here, which was set up by the owners to inform visitors of the rich history of carob in Cyprus. Carob orchards surround Mavros Chrysos and carob production was the main source of income for the community at one time. It's an evergreen and its dense broad leaves

offer welcome shade to passing travellers either on foot or needing somewhere cool to park their cars throughout the year.

The fruit looks similar to a broad bean when green but then turns brown as it matures. When my dad was a child, he and the other children would suck on the pods as a kind of sweet because they have a liquorice flavour. Once harvested the pods are dried and ground down into 'kibbles' and boiled with water, which is then strained and the remaining juice is boiled for four hours stirring constantly until it turns into a thick syrup. This is either-bottled as syrup at this stage or 'pulled' as in toffee making. When mixed with sesame seeds and sometimes peanuts it produces a type of nut brittle called PASTELLI.

The seeds of carob trees, also known as locust trees, are used to produce locust bean gum (LBG), which is used as a thickening agent in food production among other things. The seeds are remarkably uniform in weight and size regardless of the size of the pod and at one time were used as a reliable measure for the weight of gold and diamonds. The word carat being a derivative of the Greek word for carob, KERTION, which means 'horn' and describes the shape of the pod. The lone carob tree in the middle of a field is a familiar site in Cyprus, and these trees improve soil fertility. Processed carob is also used for cattle feed and the very fine carob powder is a healthy substitute for cocoa because it has a much lower fat content.

CAROB CAKE

We have already had one use of carob syrup in the wheat section with KOULOUROUTHKIA (see page 120). It is also eaten poured over fresh ANARI or anything that needs a little extra sweetness. I was sure it would taste delicious in a cake but no one had given me such a recipe and this set me thinking. My mother came from Retford in Nottinghamshire and would always make ginger parkin or gingerbread as we called it, at Christmas, as did my grandmother and now both my sister and I carry on the tradition. This is a traditional cake that uses molasses and oatmeal to make a moist dark cake, which I love and always speaks of Christmas to me. I thought that using the basic parkin recipe and substituting carob syrup for the molasses might work very well as indeed it does. I have added hazelnuts, too, as carob and hazelnuts go very well together.

75g ground hazelnuts
200g medium to fine oatmeal
200g light self-raising wholemeal flour
225g unsalted butter
225g dark Barbados sugar
2 medium/large eggs
4 generous tablespoons carob syrup
2 teaspoons baking powder
2 teaspoons ground ginger

Melt the butter gently over a low heat together with the sugar, stirring until it is dissolved, then take off the heat and stir in the carob syrup. Sift the flour into a bowl, add the oatmeal, baking powder, nuts and ginger. Whisk the eggs. Add the syrup mixture to the flour mixture and mix well, then add the eggs. Pour into a greased non-stick square (22cm) tin and bake in the oven gas mark 4/180C for 45 to 50 minutes. This cake is meant to be moist. Check by piercing the centre with a skewer and if it comes out just clean then it's cooked.

GRAPES

Vines have been cultivated in Cyprus since antiquity and, at that time, were known for their great height. Vines have been trellised since medieval times and even today both town and country houses trellis vines across their terraces to provide not only cooling shade but a few bunches of grapes either for the table or turned into wine. Trellising was mainly used in vine cultivation in the lowlands, as it allows the air to pass through the vines and protects the fruit from the intense heat of the sun. Today, when travelling between LEMESOS and PAFOS in the mountainous and semi-mountainous regions of Troodos, serried rows of stunted vines can be seen cultivated in the continental manner.

Recent archaeological evidence suggests that winemaking on Cyprus dates back 6000 years, it is even speculated that winemaking spread from Cyprus to other parts of the Mediterranean.

There are several indigenous varieties of grapes and Cyprus was among a very few countries not to be affected by the phylloxera, wine louse, which devastated crops across Europe in the 19C. The two most common grapes are the XYNESTERI, which is a white grape and the MAVRO, which is a black ancient variety also good for the table.

Cyprus has always produced a selection of excellent wines but today the wine producers are developing and extending the varieties to compete in the world market. Approximately 80 per cent of the grapes harvested go into wine production.

Grapes hold a huge bounty of possibilities and the Cypriots make full use of them, as every last scrap is utilised. The leaves are used for KOUPEPIA (see page 129). The fruit is crushed and the grape juice used to make wine, PALOUZE, SOUSHOUKO, KEFTERI and EPSIMA. The skin, pips and stalks, are distilled to make ZIVANIA, a clear strong spirit with an alcohol content of up 52 per cent. ZIVANIA is not only drunk, but also used medicinally by rubbing on the chest to relieve a cold. Caution is recommended when using this remedy, do not to go near a naked flame, particularly if you have a hairy chest; accidents have been known to occur, you have been warned!

After distillation the dross is thrown on the compost. Any leftover juice is used to make vinegar. The fruits are also dried to make raisins, which are often pierced on sticks and left in the sun to dry.

The villagers would make Commandaria, a sweet dessert wine, by crushing the grapes and leaving them in a container for 12 days to allow for fermentation after which the juice would be strained through a basket, the juice decanted with a gourd and put into a clean container. This was sealed to make it airtight and after a month the wine would be ready to taste. The indigenous grapes of Cyprus do not age well so the wine has to be drunk while young!

After all our cooking exploits with Aunt Eugenia we needed some people to help us eat the produce of our labours so Androula invited members of the family and people in the village to come and help eat it. Panayiotis, her brother, and his wife Aida were among the throng and he brought with him some of his own delicious grape juice to show me how to make PALOUZES.

PALOUZES

284ml grape juice
1 heaped dessertspoon plain flour

Mix a little grape juice with the flour to make to a smooth paste then add the rest and heat over a low flame until it thickens. At this stage it can be eaten as a cream or left to set and then cut into squares and dried in the sun, which then becomes KEFTERI. When Panayiotis and his siblings were children they loved to lick the pan and had a race to see who could finish it.

This mixture is also the basis for making SOUSHOUKO. Nuts, generally almonds but sometimes walnuts are threaded onto a string and the string is passed through the mixture then hung up to dry and the process is repeated many times until the desired thickness is reached. The finished product resembles a knobbly twig. This is then left to harden and cut into lengths and stored to be eaten throughout the winter. It is not the most attractive looking food but it has a subtle and delicious taste, which I love and it has absolutely no added sugar so it is extremely healthy. My grandmother, unusually for that area, had a big vineyard and used to make SOUSHOUKO with the grapes. My cousins remember the rows of SOUSHOUKO hanging in the yard to dry and the children hanging around the yard hoping to get a taste.

EPSIMA is grape syrup made by boiling the juice until it becomes a thick syrup and used for cooking like honey.

When buying SOUSHOUKO from a shop or stall be careful that it is made from 100 per cent grape juice. There is a cheaper variety, usually paler in colour, which has been watered down and has sugar added. The best time to buy SOUSHOUKO is in the autumn when it's fresh after the grape harvest. It is often sold at holy festivals, PANAGYRIS.

JOURNEY'S END

Exploring the recent past of Cyprus has been a fascinating journey for me. It has given me many insights into my father's background and a deeper understanding of where he was 'coming from' both literally and figuratively. I have learned a huge amount about my cultural heritage and it has answered some of my longstanding questions both large and small.

This is not a comprehensive guide to Cypriot crafts or food, or indeed life, it is a personal journey following personal interests and seeing where that took me, which was to some surprising places. I have discovered some fascinating facts about the contemporary arts and crafts in Cyprus, as well as the traditional and hopefully will continue to learn even more in the future.

I think of the Cyprus of the 1960s and '70s with nostalgia and whenever I visit I am unconsciously looking for that lost way of life still. When I see so much new development I fear that all the old buildings will eventually disappear, either torn down to make way for new development or left to fall down out of neglect. Progress has brought prosperity to many Cypriots and quality of life has improved dramatically for most but I hope this isn't at the expense of losing the character of the past or destroying the beauty of the landscape. These are the things that bring many visitors back time and time again. Ancient construction is preserved with reverence in Cyprus and now I am encouraged to see restoration of more recent old buildings in the cities and in villages, old ruins are being brought back to life. I look forward to a mixture of cherishing the old while embracing the new.

Resources

GLOSSARY

ANARI
riccotta type cheese
made from goat's or
sheep's milk

ANATHRIKA
wild fennel

ARKATENA
KOULOURIA
rusks

ARTOS
ancient Greek word
for bread

ASPROPLOUMIA
white embroidery

BAKALIAROS
salt cod

BAMIES
okra

BARBOUNI
red mullet

COLOCASSI
a species of taro

DAKTYLA
fingers

ELIES TSAKISSTES
small green cracked
olives with garlic and
coriander

ELIOPITTA
olive bread

FANGRI
king sea bream

FASOLIA
beans

FLAOUNES
pies made at Easter
time with local
cheese, eggs and
mint

FYTHKIOTIKA
type of weaving
originating from Fyti

GALATOPOUREKO
Greek sweet pastry
with milk custard
filling

GLYKO
sweet

HALLOUMI
hard goat's cheese

HALLOUMOPITTA
halloumi bread

KAFENEIA
coffee shops

KALAMARI
squid

KALON PRAMA
good thing

KAREKLA
chair

KARPOUZI
watermelon

KEFALOS
grey mullet

KERATION
horn

KOKKINOPLOUMIA
red embroidery

KOURELLOUDHES
tattered cloth

KOUPEPIA
stuffed vine leaves

KOUKIA
broad beans

KOULOURIA
bread rusk

KOUTALAKI
small spoon

KOUNOUPIDHI
cauliflower

KRASATO
a dish cooked with
red wine

LAHANA
green leafy vegetable
similar to Swiss chard

LAIKI GEITONIA
popular
neighbourhood

LAVRAKI
sea bass

LEVKARITIKA
embroidery of Levkara

LOUKOUMIA
Turkish (Greek) delight

LOUVI
black eye beans

MACARONIA TOU
FOURNOU
oven-cooked
macaroni

MARIDHA
whitebait

MASTICHA
resin crystals from the masticha tree

MAVROKOKOS
nigella sativa seeds or onion seeds

MECHLEPI
ground cherry kernels

MELITZANA
aubergine

MINERI
tunny

OCTAPODI
octopus

OSPRIA
pulses

PANAGYRI
religious festival

PANISIDA
bread used in religious observance

PANTOPOLEIO
grocer's shop (shop that sells everything)

PATATES
potatoes

PESTROFA
trout

PHIDHES
orzo pasta

PHYLLOXERA
wine louse

PIPILES
narrow knit laces

PIROUNAKI
small fork

PITHARI
large terracotta pot

PITTA
flat bread

POURGOURI
cracked wheat

POULES
young colocassi

POYATZIDES
dyers

PROSPHORON
communion bread

PSITO
roast

SAYIA
coat

SCHINOS
a small tree or bush with berries

SENDUKI
dowry chest

SKORDHALIA
garlic and bread dip

SOUPIES
cuttlefish

SOUVLA
large pieces of meat cooked over charcoal

SOUVLAKIA
small pieces of meat skewered and cooked over charcoal

SPANAKOPITA
spinach pie

STROUFOUTHKIA
a type of wild spinach

TAHINI
ground sesame seeds

TAHINOSALATA
dip made with tahini

TALARI
basket used in the making of anari

TALATTOURI
Greek word for tzatziki

TALIADOROI
ecclesiastical carvers

TARAMOSALATA
fish roe dip

TAVLI
backgammon

TO SPITIKO TOU ARCHONTA
house of the man of substance

TRAHANAS
wheat and sour milk

TREMITHIA
terebinth

TRIN
pasta

TSESTOS
flat round basket

TSEVREDES
silk embroidery

TSIPOURA
gilt head bream

TSOUREKI
Greek plaited bread

TZATZIKI
Turkish word for yoghurt,mint and cucumber dip

YEMISTA
filled or stuffed vegetables

XIDHATA
pickles

ZACHAROPLASTEIO
pastry shop

PLACES OF INTEREST

ARTS & CRAFTS

THE CYPRUS HANDICRAFT CENTRE
186 Athalassas Avenue
2025 Lefkosia, Cyprus
Tel: +357 22 305024

INIA MUSEUM
Inia, Paphos

KERAMIDEA CERAMICS
8 Nikiforou Foka Street
1016 Lefkosia, Cyprus
Tel: +357 22 430487

LEMBA POTTERY
18 Eleftherias Street, Lemba
Village, Pafos 8260, Cyprus
Tel: +357 26 270822
Email info@lembapottery.com

ODRADOR
113 Strovolos Avenue,
Apartment 201, 2042, Cyprus
Tel: +357 99 49 7857
Email rolandosl@yahoo.gr

G.ORPHANOS & CO.
10 Lykouyrgou Street,1011
Lefkosia, Cyprus
Tel: +357 22 676326

YIALOUSSA LOOM
Laiki Geitonia 1
8 Aristokyprou Street
Lefkosia, Cyprus
Tel: 02 664461

BOOKSHOPS

MOUFLON BOOKSHOP
1 Sofouli Street
1096 Lefkosia, Cyprus
POBox 22375 1521 Lefkosia,
Cyprus
Tel: +357 22 665155

MOUFLON BOOKSHOP
30 Kinyras Street
8011 Pafos, Cyprus
Tel: +357 26 934850

SOLONEION BOOK CENTRE
24 Vyzantiou Street
2064 Strovolos PO Box 24527
1300 Lefkosia, Cyprus
Tel: + 357 26 66799

PLACES TO EAT

INGA'S VEGGIE HEAVEN
Chrysalinotissa Craft Centre
2 Dimonaktos Street, Lefkosia
Tel: +357 22 344674

KLOKKOS RESTAURANT
Xylofagou, Larnaka District
Tel: +357 99 547547

AYIA ANNA'S TAVERNA
Ayia Anna
Tel: +357 22 532500

YANGOS' TAVERN
Latchi, Polis

SCORPIOS TAVERN
3 Petraki Miltiadous Street, Pafos
Tel: +357 26 934971

MUSEUMS

NICOSIA MUNICIPAL ART GALLERY
Apostolou Varnava 19, South
Nicosia, Cyprus, CY

LEVENTIS MUSEUM
Hyppocratous Street, Laiki
Geitonia. Lefkosia, Cyprus.
Tel. + 357 24 51475

PLACES TO STAY

TO SPITIKO TOU ARCHONTA
owner: Androula Christou
Treis Elies, 4846 Lemesos,
Troodos Mountains, Cyprus
Tel : 00357 9952 7117
www.spitiko3elies.com

SOURCES OF REFERENCE

BOOKS

Cyprus Folk Art by Eleni Papademetriou, (Society of Cypriot Studies & The Cyprus Folk Art Museum 1999)

Greek Cooking by Robin Howe Granada Publishing 1960

Textiles from Cyprus by Eleni Papademetriou En Tipis Publication 2008

ARTICLES & MAGAZINES

Sunjet Magazine 1994, 2000
Cyprus Mail online

PEOPLE

Androula Christou

Eleni Christofi

Mavros Chrysos Ltd. Anogyra. Limassol.

Michael Christoforou

Ioanna Christoforou

George Georgiades. Lemba Pottery, Lemba nr. Paphos

The Handicraft Service, Nicosia. Mrs Eleni

Evgenia Katsaris

Mr.Rolandos Loukaides of Odrador

Georgina Manolis Basket Museum Inea

Mr. Pilavakis

Panayiotis Trimithiotis

Aida Trimithiotis

Mrs.Avghi of Kaminaria

Mrs. Irinoula of Kaminaria

Mrs. Elpiniki of Kaminaria

Chris of Tony's Continental stores East Finchley, London.

Rosie Zisimou

WEB SITES

ARTISTS
http://noctoc-noctoc.blogspot.com

COLOCASSI
http://en.wikipedia.org/wiki/Taro

CYPRUS ON FILM
http://www.cyprusonfilm.com

CYPRUS COLLEGE OF ART
http://www.artcyprus.org/

CYPRUS MINISTRY OF COMMERCE
http://www.mcit.gov.cy

DONKEY SANCTUARY
http://drupal.thedonkeysanctuary.org.uk/view/cyprus

EDUCATION
http://education.stateuniversity.com

FLORA & FAUNA
http://factoidz.com/edible-wild-flora-and-fauna-of-the-mediterraneancyprus/

FOODS
http://www.freshfruitvegetables.com/
http://www.cyprusfoodndrinks.com

GENERAL INFORMATION
http://en.wikipedia.org

GREEN VILLAGES PROJECT
http://greenvillage.hylates-eu.com/index.php

KERAMIDEA STUDIO
http://keramideastudio.com/

LACE
www.omodos.org/users/site/english/pipila.shtm

LAONA FOUNDATION
http://www.conservation.org.cy/laona/laona.htm

MASTICHA
http://www.chios.gr/products/mastic.htm

NICOSIA MUNICIPAL ART CENTRE
http://www.nimac.org.cy

POTTERY
www.cypruspotteryassociation.info

TREIS ELIES
http://www.triselies.org

WEAVING
http://phitiotika.files.wordpress.com

WINES
http://www.winesofcyprus.co.uk
http://www.cypruswineries.org/

INDEX